THE OPERATED JEW

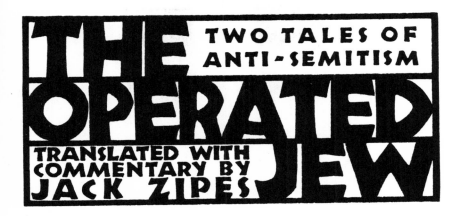

THE OPERATED JEW

TWO TALES OF ANTI-SEMITISM

TRANSLATED WITH COMMENTARY BY JACK ZIPES

ROUTLEDGE

NEW YORK AND LONDON

Published in 1991 by
Routledge
An imprint of Routledge, Chapman and Hall, Inc.
29 West 35 Street
New York, NY 10001

Published in Great Britain by
Routledge
11 New Fetter Lane
London EC4P 4EE

Library of Congress Cataloging-in-Publication Data

Zipes, Jack David.
    The operated Jew / Jack Zipes.
       p. cm.
    Includes bibliographical references and index.
    ISBN 0-415-90460-9. — ISBN 0-415-90461-7 (pbk.)
    1. Antisemitism—Germany. 2. Jews—Germany—Cultural assimilation. 3. Jews in literature. 4. Panizza, Oskar, 1853–1921—Criticism and interpretation. 5. Friedlaender, Salomo, 1871–1946—Criticism and interpretation. 6. Germany—Ethnic relations.
I. Title.
DS146.G4Z57   1991
943'.004924—dc20   91-23709
                                        CIP

British Library of Congress data also available

for my mother
Celia Zipes

These revisions of the past are probably even less trustworthy than
    our random, everyday assemblages
and have most likely even more to do with present unknowables, so
    I offer this almost in passing,
with nothing, no moral distillation, no headily pressing imperatives
    meant to be lurking beneath it.
I wonder, putting it most simply, leaving out humiliation, anything
    like that, if I might have been their Jew?
I wonder, I mean, if I might have been an implement for them, not
    of atonement—I'd have nosed that out—
but of absolution, what they'd have used to get them shed of some-
    thing rankling—history, it would be:
they'd have wanted to be categorically and finally shriven of it, or
    of that part of it at least
which so befouled the rest, which so acutely contradicted it with
    glory and debasement.

                            C.K. Williams, *Combat* (1983)

The past does not cast its light on the present, nor the present on the
past. Rather, it is in the image that the past comes together with the
now like lightning to form a constellation. In other words, the image
is the dialectic in stillstand. Indeed, while the connection of the present
to the past is a purely temporal and continuous one, the connection of
the past to the now is dialectical. It is not the course of time but image,
volatile.—Only dialectical images are genuine (this means, not archaic)
images. And the place where one encounters them is language.—Awakening—

                    Walter Benjamin, *Das Passagen-Werk* (1927–40)

Contents

Acknowledgments

About ten years ago Andy Rabinbach and I edited a series of special issues on Germans and Jews for *New German Critique*. This book emanated from that project, and Andy's incisive questions have continued to help me rethink some of the crucial notions in my present work. In different ways, I have also been strongly influenced by Dan Diner, Frank Stern, and Sander Gilman, who have dealt with issues pertinent to my project. Moreover, I am particularly indebted to Andy Markovits and Moishe Postone, who read with great care an early draft of the introduction and took me to task when necessary. Their criticism has made me revise some of my fundamental assumptions about the German-Jewish symbiosis. I have also benefited from discussions about Jewish identity and politics with Charlie Williams, who is the hidden muse behind this work. Last but not least I would like to express my special gratitude to a special editor, Bill Germano, who has always been willing to take risks and go out on a limb for me.

My translation of Oskar Panizza's "The Operated Jew" and my essay "Oskar Panizza: The Operated German as Operated Jew" first appeared in *New German Critique* in 1980. Both have been revised for this book.

A Note on Georg Grosz's Painting "Dedication to Oskar Panizza"

Painted during 1917–18, Grosz's "Dedication to Oskar Panizza" represents a constellation of the techniques and themes he had developed during the war years. Through his collage he brings together bestial human figures from different times and places to create a futuristic hell reminiscent of the paintings of Bosch and Breughel. The priest as the principle of morality appears helpless in the face of the depraved figures symbolizing alcoholism, syphillis, war, and plague. Grosz wrote in a letter of 1917 that he wanted his painting to express his protest against the insanity that had overcome humanity during World War II. He dedicated his painting to Panizza because he believed that Panizza had placed his finger on the destructive and hellish tendencies of this period. Interestingly, Salomo Friedlaender admired Grosz's work very much and wrote a monograph entitled *Georg Grosz* (1922), in which he extolled Grosz's use of the grotesque to depict the distorted polarities in the world.

Preliminary Diagnosis

I spent most of 1990 in Europe, and as an American Jew, I was marked by what I read, saw, and experienced. Skinheads forming swastikas every Saturday on Alexanderplatz in "liberated" East Berlin, while the police calmly observed the scene without interfering. A Jewish cemetery in Carpentras, France, desecrated, bodies disinterred, and other anti-Semitic acts covertly performed in a country where, since 1979, a professor by the name of Faurisson has openly denied that the Nazi death camps ever existed. The resurgence of anti-Semitism in Poland, despite the fact that there are only ten thousand Jews left of the approximately three million before 1940. Soviet Jews eager to leave the Soviet Union because of widespread anti-Semitic attacks. Israelis beating and killing Palestinians while welcoming Soviet Jews to their "Homeland." Then, finally, back in America, the assassination of Rabbi Meir Kahane, a proponent of violence and intolerance brought down by the sickness he actively sought to cultivate and spread. The result: more

1

murders of Palestinians followed by murders of Israelis. Meanwhile, the peaceful Germans, who helped build the factories producing biological-chemical weapons both in Iraq and Libya, sent millions of dollars worth of food to the Soviet Union and supported the Desert Shield troops in Saudi Arabia with more millions and materials so that the Desert Storm Troops could eventually mount a victorious *Blitzkrieg*.

For Germans, the year 1990 marked the culmination of a long struggle to become unified again, free as one *Volk,* the most powerful economic nation in the world, achieving ironically through peace a partial fulfillment of Hitler's dream of a great empire. For Jews, the year 1990 marked a year of shame in which the Israelis as representatives of Jews throughout the world continued to oppress Palestinians, bringing Israel through violence closer to the brink of destruction and sowing discord among Jews all over the world.[1]

What will historians make of the "historical" year 1990? Have we celebrated the rise of a New Europe too soon? What role will the Jews be *assigned* in this New Europe dominated by Germany? And by whom?

Ernst Bloch, the German-Jewish philosopher of hope, once said that the Marxist dictum about history never repeating itself is false. Wherever and whenever history is not grasped radically, that is, seized by its roots, it will surely repeat itself. And certainly, despite all the penetrating books written about the causes and consequences of the Holocaust, despite the depictions of and reportage about the Nazis and worldwide collusion regarding anti-Semitism, the official pronouncements by the Catholic Church that the Jews did not after all kill Christ, the grandiose admissions of guilt by the West German government, and reparations paid to Jewish refugees and to the Israeli government, the historical lessons of the Holocaust have been grasped neither by the gentile nor by the Jewish world.

History must be written with the dead in mind. What is new can never be new unless the dead are truly buried and mourned. What is new can only bring redemption if it is not a perverse form of the old. But redemption can only occur, I am convinced, if graves are turned over and ghosts exhumed, ghosts like Oskar Panizza and Salomo Friedlaender: two writers as different as night and day, yet similarly haunted and persecuted by religious and racist fanaticism in Germany. Their only means of defense was through the pen, a warped pen, producing macabre and grotesque stories of mutilation and horror and thrashing diatribes against German hypocrisy and imperiousness. Together they form a dialectical image—the operated Jew/German—which in turn casts images onto the present, illustrating why we devastate our bodies in quest for purity and perfection. At least, so it seems to me, for throughout the year 1990 I was haunted by images from their stories and by reflections about their lives. I felt that I had to return to them to grasp the virulent rise of anti-Semitism in Europe and the violence of the Israelis and Arabs in the Middle East. All these events appeared to be historically contingent on a modern constellation of racist and utopian tendencies in advanced industrial societies at the end of the nineteenth century. They struck me as disturbingly familiar, defying comprehension despite their familiarity, because their "nowness," what Walter Benjamin called the *Jetztzeit*, has not been adequately depicted in an image that could stand still in our minds. As he remarked in his *Theses on the Philosophy of History:*

> The true picture of the past flits by. The past can be seized only as an image which flashes up at the instant when it can be recognized and is never seen again. "The truth will not run away from us": in the historical outlook of historicism these words of Gottfried Keller mark the exact point where historical materialism

cuts through historicism. For every image of the past that is not recognized by the present as one of its own concerns threatens to disappear irretrievably.[2]

Whatever was and is the "now" about the new anti-Semitism and the operations of the Israelis could only be fathomed, I thought, through a metaphor of the past, or rather metaphors both bizarre and grotesque, so that perhaps the incredible and unspeakable present, our "nowness," might become more credible, more speakable.

The grotesque tales *The Operated Jew* (1893) and *The Operated Goy* (1922) by Panizza and Mynona (Friedlaender's pseudonym) speak to the *new* anti-Semitism in Europe. But more than that, they are icons of "the Holocaust and modernity," to quote the title of a thoughtful book by Zygmunt Bauman.[3] Too often the Holocaust has been used to rationalize Jewish and Israeli interests, or to evoke emotional responses that cloud the meaning of the extermination of European Jewry. The Holocaust has become a designation turned against itself, depleted of its historical meaning; all kinds of annihilation are associated with it ranging from the mass slaughter in Cambodia to the devastation of one football team by another and most recently to the massive bombing of Baghdad during the Desert Storm operation in 1991. The term Holocaust has even been used against Jews themselves to characterize Israeli aggression and to cast aspersions on Israel, or in graffiti and jokes to expose the hatred of Jews. In short, its uniqueness has been leveled by language and changed attitudes since 1945, resulting in a repression and perversion of its ramifications for the present: the Holocaust has been made into a *common* aberration like a temporary upheaval in the weather. We can live with aberrations likened to storms because we know they will pass and believe that they are not caused by normal people but by conditions seemingly beyond our control, driving normal people crazy. Therefore, if the Holocaust was unique in its own time, it has now (after the storm) been deemed meaningless because we have been led to believe that it was an aberration that can make anyone disturbed and brutal at one time or another, including Jews themselves.

But Bauman's work refuses to allow us to obliterate the uniqueness of the Holocaust in this way. He recaptures its singular meaning by focusing on specific developments in the Western civilizing process itself that brought about the Holocaust, and demonstrates how we continue to violate its unique signification by rationally normalizing it. According to Bauman, three important developments had to converge by the beginning of the twentieth century to prepare the way for the Holocaust: the anti-Semitic conceptualization of the Jew; the legitimization of racism as a science; the displacement of morality through the worship of social engineering and rational management of society.

During the course of the nineteenth century, the basis of anti-Semitism was changed from religious discrimination to a racial and political hatred of all Jews, now conceptualized as diseased, non-conformist, demonic, subversive, and anomalous. The homeless Jew, emancipated during the nineteenth century, was metaphorized as viscous or slimy, everywhere at the same time, insidiously dissolving the pure fabric of society. The conceptual Jew was born. It was this Jew who was made to exist in the minds of many Westerners through the cooperative efforts of church and state and the various institutions of a public sphere that nurtured Judeophobia.

Given the changed socio-political conditions, Jews had to be concretely described as a race, stigmatized by their names and tell-tale features. While they were being stamped with racial features and characteristics, racism itself became legitimized as a science. During the latter part of the nineteenth century, numerous studies were written to prove that there were great differences among the races and that some were superior to others and deserved to inherit the earth—the entire earth—so that the perfect society might come about. The result, as Bauman insightfully remarks, is that racism came to

> stand apart by a practice of which it is a part and which it rationalizes, a practice that combines strategies of architecture and gardening with that of medicine—in the service of the construction of an artificial social order, through cutting out the elements of the present reality that neither fit the visualized perfect reality, nor can be changed so that they do. In a world that boasts the unprecedented ability to improve human conditions by reorganizing human affairs on a rational basis, racism manifests the conviction that a certain category of human beings cannot be incorporated into the rational order, whatever the effort. . . . To use the medical metaphor; one can train and shape "healthy" parts of the body, but not cancerous growth. The latter can be "improved" only by being destroyed.[4]

The technology to improve while destroying, to perfect while eliminating, reached unimaginable heights during the first part of the twentieth century. In the name of the civilizing process and progress, science undermined traditional morality by establishing rational calculation and domination of nature as ideals by which to measure oneself and the advance of society. The goals of "civilized" members of Western societies, those who had been indoctrinated into the rational and functional division of labor, were to reinforce bodily self-control and cultural inhibitions of close bodily contact and to create segregated and isolated territories free of violence, models of the perfect advanced technological society.

It is no wonder that the Holocaust became feasible: the Nazi endeavor to create a perfect Aryan society, *Judenrein,* a state purified of Jews and other diseased elements, was in keeping with the other fascist, communist, and even democratic experiments throughout most of the Western world to create the perfect society in keeping with the norms of social engineering. In fact, the opposition to the Nazis was not based on the cruel and inhumane way they began operating on the Jews. On the contrary, the Nazis could have continued, rationally and legally, to remove Jews and cleanse their country of Jews if they had not overstepped the boundaries of acceptable imperialism. Even when World War II erupted, the Jews were treated by the Allied forces as disruptive and bothersome objects in their field of operations. The war, as we know, was not a war in defense of Jews.[5] It was not until *after* 1945, until after six million Jews were dead and the autopsies began, that the world began to view the Jews as more than concepts. The acknowledgment of the Holocaust briefly turned them into humans, who were allowed to establish their own state, where they, like other peoples, could begin civilizing themselves and create their own version of a perfect society, making a garden out of the desert.

Yet, many rabid anti-Semites and anti-Zionists view Israel as nothing but a cancerous growth.[6]

Recall Bauman's medical metaphor: "One can train and shape 'healthy' parts of the body, but not cancerous growth. The latter can be 'improved' only by being destroyed." This chilling trope reveals how Jews are still the subject of multiple operations, and how these operations exemplify the dangers inherent in the social engineering of modernity, dangers not solely for Jews, but for all minority groups, for all peoples subjected to discrimination, disassociated from the so-called normal by rational categories which designate and stigmatize.[7]

The West has become obsessed by cleansing its body and keeping it "free" from disease. This obsession is apparent on both a personal and social level. For example, the fear of all kinds of diseases and of aging has led to our endeavor to make our bodies function like smooth-running machines and to replace parts whenever they degenerate. The fear of other cultures and other peoples depicted as aliens intruding into the sanctity of our nation and violating the norms of our public spheres has led us to give the state more police powers leading to legitimated violence in the name of rational management of society. We are forever on the lookout for cancerous growths.

Israel has been likened to a cancerous growth.

Of course, there are other kinds of unfortunate cancerous growths, but I am concerned here primarily with the necessity of operating on Jews. I am concerned with the image of the operated Jew/German, because it has great ramifications for "the new world order" that, we are told, is presently taking shape.

After 1948, Israel embodied the Jews, all Jews, even the majority, who continued to live in the diaspora. Israel was the *body of the Jews*. And though it may have seemed a perfectly healthy body to the Israelis, who turned the desert into a garden, and to the diaspora Jews, who supported the Israeli experiments, Israel was viewed by the Arabs as an infected implant, and as a corporeal donation by the United Nations. In fact, however, it was nothing more than a convenient dumping ground, where the so-called "United Nations" sought to discard their weeds of shame. Nobody expected or really wanted Israel to thrive, not unless, that is, its role could be assigned, unless Jews could continue to serve as the malignant disease, diverting attention from the irrational and inhumane forces of social engineering that helped propel capitalist development in the West and communist domination in the East.

Paradoxically, the Jews could only become victims again if they were operated on and transformed into Nazis. Grotesque as this may seem, this operation began taking place as a new form of anti-Semitism arose in the post-Holocaust period. This new anti-Semitism is clearly political and follows the first two phases of religious and racist anti-Semitism, while drawing upon the stereotypes and prejudices of the earlier phases for its foundation. In contrast to the anti-Semitism before the Holocaust, which really did not need a real race or religion to become rampant, the conceptualization of the Jew as Nazi demands a concrete Jew as Zionist. Or, in other words, this anti-Semitism could not exist without the real existence of the state of Israel, the Jewish body. Furthermore, it emanates from that German-Jewish symbiosis which, even today, has a bearing on the fate of Jews in Europe and the Middle East and is symptomatic of the modernity of the Holocaust.

Until recently very little has been written about the relations between Germans and Jews in Germany since 1945,[8] as though Hitler had indeed accomplished his goal of purifying Germany of Jews. Furthermore, it has generally been assumed that no self-respecting Jew would have wanted to live in Germany after the Holocaust. However, Hitler never did realize the Final Solution, and many Jews, who survived the Holocaust, decided to stay in Germany after 1945; others were "displaced" there by chance and remained because of lack of opportunities to emigrate. Whatever their reasons may have been, thousands of Jews did make their home in West and East Germany. Gradually, the re-formation of their ties to the Germans, who repressed their crimes against the Jews through guilt and silence and heavy reparations paid to Israel and individual Jews, has led to the newest form of anti-Semitism, which conceptualizes the operated Jew as potential Nazi. Certainly, the Germans are not the sole perpetrators of this new anti-Semitism, nor are most Germans anti-Semitic. But the very fact that this conception of the Jew as potential Nazi has become visible in Germany reveals how grotesque the German-Jewish symbiosis has become. Some critics like Gerschom Scholem have denied that there ever was a German-Jewish symbiosis in the first place. According to Scho-

lem, the Jewish enthusiasm for German culture and their partici-
pation in it was always one-sided and unreciprocated. Their
relationship was "never anything else than a fiction"[9] that had
disastrous results for the Jews because it denied the possibility of
emancipation. The considerable debate surrounding Scholem's
remarks has never been resolved.[10] However, as Dan Diner has
cogently demonstrated, it is extremely clear that a German-
Jewish symbiosis has indeed developed *since* 1945:

> Since Auschwitz—what a sad, ironic twist—one can indeed
> speak about a "German-Jewish symbiosis." Of course, it is a
> negative one: for both, for Germans as well as for Jews, the result
> of the mass annihilation has become the starting point for their
> self-comprehension. It is a kind of contradictory mutuality,
> whether they want it or not, for Germans as well as Jews have
> been linked to one another anew through this event. Such a
> negative symbiosis, constituted by the Nazis, will stamp the rela-
> tionship of each group to itself, and above all, each group to
> another for generations to come.[11]

Aside from the fact that the history of the post-Holocaust
German-Jewish symbiosis can reveal, for Germans and Jews
alike, a great deal about the problematics of national and cultural
identity in contemporary Germany, it is also highly significant
in general because this history contains elements of the new anti-
Semitism that can be found in the present "New Europe" and
helps explain the rise of the Jews' own self-conception of the
"tough Jew." Since this is a chapter of history that I have personally experienced, I want to outline here the major contours of
this new anti-Semitism as I have seen it develop in relation to
the operated Jew/German. My view may, therefore, be somewhat
myopic. But historians will, I hope, deal in more depth with this
chapter, correct my vision, and dig further into taboo ground.

◆

The problem of anti-Semitism in Germany after 1945 was so immense that the Allied forces found themselves incapable of dealing with it. In fact, at the very beginning they even respected the anti-Semitic legislation of the Nazis and even used German police and guards to "watch over" the Jewish refugees in the camps of displaced persons.[12] Moreover, the Germans, suffering from the ravages of the war, were unwilling on the one hand to return property and goods to their rightful Jewish owners and on the other psychologically unwilling to take the Jews back into their midst because they held them responsible for the German defeat and shame. In short, anti-Semitism did not end in Germany in 1945. Though the Jews tried to reclaim their rights and demanded recognition as citizens, and though 230,000 spent some time in Germany between 1945 and 1948, they were basically encouraged to disappear and leave Germany if not Europe. Neither the denazification program of the Occupation forces nor the gradual help provided by the military government enabled the Jews to be at home in Germany. Instead, they were made to feel as though they themselves were still a problem. In other words, there was no German problem after the war but another nagging Jewish problem. This problem was treated in two different ways when the two new German states were officially founded in 1949. Yet, neither treatment cured the Germans of their anti-Semitic sentiments. Rather both led toward a new form of political anti-Semitism with parallels that can be drawn to the perpetuation of Judeophobia in the Communist bloc countries and the free West at large.

In the German Democratic Republic, the entire question of anti-Semitism was practically negated once the state was formed. Part of the legitimization process of the Communist Party (the SED) was to portray communists as the "true" resisters and victims of fascism. The extermination of the Jews was tragic, but only minor compared to the killing of seventeen million Soviet soldiers and citizens, not to mention the murder of German communists by the Nazis. Such a policy was very much in keeping with the anti-Semitism of the Stalin regime. With the support of the Soviets, the German Democratic Republic refused to pay any sort of reparation to Israel after 1949, nor did it recognize Israel as a legitimate state. After all, why should the victims of fascism, namely the communists, pay other victims for crimes that they, the communists, did not commit? Recognition of Israel was likened to recognition of guilt.

Such state policy was cathartic for the fifteen million Germans, who constituted the East German state, but it also led to their denial of complicity in crimes against the Jews. If they could rehabilitate themselves as loyal followers of communism, they would not have to feel shame for their crimes, their Judeophobia, or the Nazi past. Instead, they could rationally *distance* themselves from the atrocities of World War II and insert themselves into a new social order that had as its goal the perfection of the world in the name of communism.

During the next forty years, the East Germans barely had to trouble themselves about anti-Semitism; they were absolved of this prejudice as long as they believed in communism and the State.[13] The German Democratic Republic made no effort whatsoever to include passages about the Holocaust in the history books about contemporary German and European history. Moreover, since censorship was extensive throughout East Germany, there were very few novels or plays that dealt with the Holocaust or Jews. In short by the early 1960s, the State had successfully kept the sparks of latent anti-Semitism alive in East Germany by negating the role played by Germans in the Holocaust and by minimizing the Holocaust itself.

Given such a policy, it is no wonder that very few Jews chose to remain in East Germany after 1949. At most, there may have been 3,000 Jews at one time. By 1989 this number had dwindled to less than 1,000, most of whom lived in East Berlin. Those Jews who had decided to remain in East Germany were mainly assimilated, Jews with a strong commitment to Communism and often privileged members of the Party. Others were Eastern European Jews who became stranded there and found a certain amount of security in becoming anonymous. Very few were religious. Outside East Berlin there were no synagogues, no effective Jewish pressure groups, no means to voice one's concerns as a Jew. In fact, Jews like Christians were encouraged to become Party members or atheists. It seemed an easy operation, almost a miracle: simply by becoming a Communist, a Jew could transform himself or herself into a German without being killed.

The pressures for Jews in East Germany to become non-Jews and anonymous were increased after the Seven Day War in 1967. From that point on, Israel was constantly depicted as a Zionist imperialist state, one that simply represented the interests of the United States in the Middle East. Whenever *Neues Deutschland,* the official daily newspaper of the Party, wrote about Israel, it was always in association with imperialism and Zionism if not fascism. But Zionism had become a code name for anti-Semitism, for Israelis were equated with Jews all over the world. The East Germans, who knew almost no Jews, still had their dormant prejudices: the Jew existed for them again, re-conceptualized as imperialist, fascist, aggressor, and victimizer. Indeed, Jews in East Germany could deny any association with "Jewishness" by attacking the Zionism of the Israelis (as the remarkable novelist Jurek Becker once did);[14] they could repress the anti-Semitism by ignoring the anti-Semitic implications of the harsh criticism of Israel and the Israelis; they could try to leave. But they could not dare to be Jewish, at least, not in any open way.

It was not until the late 1980s, following the awakening of a new German-Jewish consciousness in West Germany, that the several hundred Jews left in East Berlin began resisting the anti-

Semitism in East Germany. Many of the younger Jews tried to become religious again; others sought to reacquaint themselves with Jewish culture. The state, under pressure from West Germany and outside Jewish organizations, even gave money for the upkeep of the Jewish cemeteries and the maintenance of a meeting place. And once the government collapsed in 1989, Israel was promised reparations. Declarations were even made about the Nazi past and the negligence of the German Democratic Republic in dealing with the Holocaust and questions of anti-Semitism.

But it was too late. The skinheads were dancing on Alexanderplatz with their swastikas. Most East Germans know no other Jews except Zionist imperialists and some who were even high ranking members of their own Communist Party like Markus Wolf, the head of the East German secret police.[15] Whatever the case may be, the image of the Jew that developed in East Germany recalls Nazism, but not the Nazism of the Germans, who were part of their heritage and committed atrocious crimes against the Jews.

This image of the Jew is somewhat different in West Germany, but not much different. Certainly now with the reunification of Germany a consensus is being formed, but it is one that will not work in the favor of the Jews, whose history may be forgotten or may become obliterated in the name of nationalism.

From the beginning, the official policy of West Germany, also known as the Federal Republic of Germany, had to be pro-Jewish. Or, put another way, West Germany could not use Communism to negate the role that Germans played in the Holocaust; it accepted the notion of collective guilt and responsibility. The West German government gradually instituted a program of reparations for Israel and for individual Jews that amounted to millions of dollars. Israeli-German friendship societies were organized in the 1950s. Special trade agreements were reached with Israel. Jews living in Germany had special licenses to sell certain commodities at discount rates. Property was returned to rightful owners. Losses were rectified. However, the reaction to the official philo-Semitic policies of the State was mixed.[16] The majority of the Germans did not support either special treatment for the Jews or reparations. Indicative of German attitudes is the following account filed by a small group of American Jews, members of the Anti-Defamation League of B'nai B'rith, invited in 1954 by the government of the Federal Republic to interview Germans from different classes and groups and to become acquainted with conditions in West Germany.

We found troubled consciences in Germany only among the comparatively few who somehow had escaped the evil and all-encompassing embrace of the Third Reich. As for the "average" German, we, too, found his conscience terrifyingly good. We could detect no deep-seated neuroses, for instance, among those at a political meeting we attended in Bad Godesberg. It was a meeting of the Gesamtdeutscher Bloc, one of the smaller German parties, called for our edification to discuss the "Jewish Question." The group has the dubious distinction of having proportionately more former Nazis among its 500,000 members than any other party in the country. This particular unit is headed by a man truly eager "to make peace with the Jews," and our presence in Germany was his opportunity for what he termed "a frank discussion." One hundred men and women filled the *Bierstube* in which the meeting was held, and there wasn't a neurotic tic among them. They were perhaps startled to be faced by 'the Jewish question' in the presence of American Jews, but they rose quickly to the occasion unhampered by burdensome feelings of guilt. . . . Through the evening the explanations continued. Here and there, we heard a comment of regret, but none of contrition. Among those average Germans—craftsmen, white collar workers, factory hands, minor professionals—there seemed to be no understanding that the rejection of which one of their number spoke had led to hatred and hatred to murder—the murder of six million. Nor did they indicate any deep personal involvement in the tragedy. They were not of the stuff of which neurotics are made. Indeed, when our own spokesman sat down after a 20 minute impassioned response to their cold explanations, the leader of the group turned in hearty friendliness to say: *"When two fellows fight and one wins and the other loses, the winner should walk up to the loser, put his arm around his shoulder and say: 'Come, let's make up.' The Germans lost; the Jews won. Now that it is all behind us, shouldn't the Jews make some gesture of friendship to the Germans."*[17]

Such a reaction was not surprising. The government had done very little in practice to combat the old anti-Semitism of the Nazis and their supporters. The reason why the majority of the Germans did not want to indemnify the Jews was that most did not feel involved in the Holocaust and claimed that they had known nothing about the concentration camps. And, in fact, for most Germans, this was true to a certain extent. After all, the Jews were legally removed from their homes during the 1940s, transported like cattle in closed cars, and exterminated for the most part *outside* of Germany. Still, if their new democratic government asserted that enough Germans as Nazis had been involved in crimes against Jews and that theirs was a moral responsibility for the Holocaust, then, as law-abiding citizens, the Germans would pay. But they would resent the payments, the guilt, the shame, and especially the Jews, who caused all of this. They would also resent the hypocritical policy of the government, because they knew that the Bonn administration of Konrad Adenauer did very little to rid the public institutions of Jew killers and anti-Semites, and that some of Adenauer's ministers and advisers had played a vital role in the Nazi cause. As I have already remarked, German post-war history has yet to be written from the perspective of the German-Jewish symbiosis, but when it is, that study will be obliged to demonstrate how German anti-Semitism was maintained under the official guise of philo-Semitism. The Germans wanted to rebuild and to forget the war. They did not want to feel threatened or guilty and needed institutional guarantees in exchange for their obedience that their suffering would be kept to a minimum. Therefore, most of the judges who had played crucial roles in enforcing the Nazi laws continued working for the new democratic government. Most of the teachers and professors who had educated and guided the Hitler youth retained their jobs. Most of the leading industrialists, excepting those who had committed flagrant crimes, reassumed their positions. With the financial support of the American Marshall Plan, the Federal Republic underwent the "economic miracle" of the 1950s and was soon functioning *normally* again. That is, normative behavior was determined by compliance with the operational rules and regulations of the new democratic Constitution and the institutions of the public sphere that basically reinforced the capitalist economy. As I have emphasized, these institutions, which had been authoritarian, were only slightly modified in character. Their major function was to guarantee that socialization would create an effective work force loyal to the new democracy which in turn owed its stability mainly to the success of advanced technology and material achievement.

The socialization of Germans during the 1950s and 1960s did not include educating them about anti-Semitism, that is, about the thinking and behavior that contributed to Judeophobia. The purpose of socialization was to develop "democratic" Germans, who were to be protected from the immediate past by minimizing the traumatic effects it might have on the young. Democratization meant "Americanization," which, in turn, led to an idolization of American popular music, films, material goods, and

power. The Germans' absorption in the American culture indus-
try became a diversion, especially for the young, so that part of
their socialization in the "new" civilizing process meant the
encouragement of collective amnesia. Very few Nazi killers were
brought to trial in the German courts during the 1950s and
1960s. History books did not deal with the Holocaust, and
students rarely studied contemporary history any way. Former
concentration camps like Dachau were transformed into tiny
sterile museums, which few Germans ever visited. The subject
of the Jews and their wartime experiences was taboo in most
German families. Moreover, it was difficult to obtain a clear idea
of what it meant to be a Jew and what Judaism was since there
were so few Jews in West Germany, and those who existed
seemed to be anonymous. Jews blended in with Germans. Or so
it seemed.

Indeed, for the most part, the Jews did try to blend into the
German landscape—out of fear. By the early 1950s there were
approximately 30,000 registered Jews mainly in the large cities
of Frankfurt, Munich, West Berlin, and Hamburg. (In Germany,
each individual is obliged to list one's religion for tax purposes,
since Germans pay taxes to support the churches and synagogues.) These Jews, and perhaps a few thousand others, who
registered as atheists, were not now inclined to make themselves
noticeable. Most of these Jews were not "German" Jews, but
came from Eastern Europe; from 1945–1950, the period of
emigration to Israel, the United States, South America, and other
western countries, they became stranded in West Germany for
one reason or another. Though there were economic benefits for
most Jews who could prove they had been victimized by the
Nazis, psychological pressures affected all Jews. Not only were
the Jews fearful of revealing their Jewish identity, they also felt
shame for staying in Germany. During the 1950s, international
and American Jewish organizations attacked all Jews who re-

mained in Germany. As a result, the "new" German Jews often felt themselves to be sinners and traitors. Finally, since West Germany actively recruited Jews to return or stay in Germany in order to show to the world how tolerant the Germans had become, many Jews also felt as though they had become objects for display.

Until the late 1960s, it was officially good to be Jewish in West Germany, but the good Jew was the silent and unobtrusive Jew. It was also good for Germans to be philo-Semitic and pro-Israel just as long as Jews were still considered to be victims and Israel was far away and threatened with extinction by the Arabs. To identify with the Jews was to identify oneself as a victim. And this was one of the prime reasons why so many young Germans began visiting Israel in the 1950s and 1960s, for those Germans born during and right after the war were to a large extent "victimized" by their parents who expected them to understand and overcome a past hung around their necks like an albatross and never explained to them. Yet, the victimization went deeper than even they realized. In my opinion, though sincere contrition was expressed by many young Germans, it was also mixed with philo-Semitism, which concealed an irrational resentment toward Jews, who were to blame for the excruciating repression in their own families, the loss of German lives, and the sense of moral guilt they were compelled to bear without ever really knowing why. At the same time, many of the young Jews, born after the Holocaust, started coming of age during the early 1960s, at the point when there were signs that the "goodness" associated with being a Jew—that is, their silence—might be broken. The negative symbiosis was bound to lead to a dramatic polarization.

Actually, at the very beginning of the 1960s, there had already been disturbing signs indicating that the Holocaust and anti-Semitism could not be entirely repressed in Germany, and that philo-Semitism could not rationalize anti-Semitism among Germans. The first and most important public event that concerned the Holocaust did not actually take place on German soil but in Israel—the Eichmann Trial of 1961–62. Nevertheless, it was telecast and covered by the German news media almost every day, making Germans more conscious of the extermination of the Jews and of how well-organized the murder machine had been. In addition to the dramatic "spectacle" of this trial, a series of plays were produced in German theaters that dealt with controversial topics pertaining to the Holocaust. Max Frisch's *Andorra* (1961) depicted how a hypocritical society could force a non-Jew to become victimized as a Jew when he is cast into that role; Rolf Hochhuth's *The Deputy* (1963) brought charges against Pope Pius XII and the Catholic Church for aiding and abetting the Nazi extermination of the Jews; Peter Weiss's *The Investigation* (1965) was a documentary drama based on the Frankfurt trial against 21 persons charged with committing crimes at Auschwitz. Weiss's play opened at nine different theaters in West Germany and was staged in such a way that contemporary Germans were implicated in the crimes of Auschwitz.

Needless to say, all these plays (and there were others) caused Germans and Jews uneasy feelings and stimulated greater public discussion about the Nazi past. In addition, more pressure was placed on the West German government to prosecute Nazi criminals, and it responded by placing more ex-Nazis on trial after 1965 than it had tried in the twenty years since the termination of World War II. However, the Seven Days War in 1967 was to bring about a strange turn of events and attitudes.

Up until 1967, it appeared that the dissatisfaction of the younger Germans with the authoritarian institutions and behavior of their parents would lead them to break open the sealed chambers of Nazism to ascertain the "truth" about the past which had become their burden. Obviously, the events of the Nazi period had not been aired enough in the family and in public, and the repression was leading the young Germans, who had a strong interest in democracy, to address the question of Nazism. Yet, the more one talked about fascism, the less one talked about anti-Semitism and the Holocaust; this was particularly true of the young German students of the New Left. The destructive, totalitarian nature of Nazism was associated more with the military industrial complex of capitalism, and so the student movement focused on capitalism and/or imperialism as the true enemies of modern civilization. Significantly, the outbreak of the student movement began in June of 1967 when a student was killed in Berlin during a protest against the visit of the Shah of Iran, considered a puppet of the United States. Thereafter, West German students sought to support the oppressed Iranians against U.S. imperialism that was also on the rise in Vietnam. Then, in the summer of 1967, following the victory of the Israelis and the occupation of the West Bank and the Gaza Strip, it was also apparent that US imperialism, which supported Israel, was being maintained by the Israelis.

It is perhaps one of the most ironic features of the German student movement, which sought to overcome the Nazi past and bring about a more genuine democratic if not socialist Germany by dealing with the remnants of totalitarianism, that it fell prey to a key element of the new anti-Semitism, beginning to spread in Europe and the United States—anti-Zionism, which became a code word for all kinds of Judeophobia. It is possible to argue that anti-Zionism began as *unintentional* anti-Semitism, for the critics of the Israeli politics were at first concerned about the ramifications of the occupation of Palestinian territory for the situation in the Middle East. Actually, in the beginning, the more conservative Germans rejoiced in the Israeli victory; up to that point the Israelis had been the underdogs in the Middle East, and the reactionary forces in Germany enjoyed empathizing with the "tough Jews," as if through them the days of the *Blitzkrieg* could be relived. This was not the case with the German students on the Left, who identified with the Arabs as victims, as though this identification might absolve them of the guilt they felt about the Nazi past. The more the Israelis took the offensive in the Middle East and the more they oppressed the Palestinians, the more they became associated with imperialism. Nor was it just the leftist students who made this association. Across the entire spectrum of German politics, old anti-Semitic sentiments could be noticed in the guise of anti-Zionism. Rhetorical questions were posed and suppositions asserted. How did Israel get the money to build up its army if it were not for Jewish capital that resided in the United States? Wasn't it obvious by the Israeli expansion that there was a Jewish conspiracy to take over the world? Isn't it apparent that the Jews think they are a superior race by the way they are treating and exterminating the Arabs? Somehow these questions kept leading to a strange but logical equation: Jews = oppressors = Nazis. All this was borne out in the fall of 1982 by the role played by the Israelis in the massacres of Palestinians in Sabra and Schatilla. The Jews revealed who they are.

Very rarely do Germans make distinctions among Jews. They are uncomfortable with the word *Jude* because it is so loaded and was, until 1945, literally a curse word, a stigma. It is interesting to note that Jews in Germany are legally referred to as *Israeliten* (Israelites). For most younger Germans, all Jews are euphemistically Israelites, and ironically this euphemism played into the new political anti-Semitism that developed during the late 1960s: the equation of all Jews with Israelis. Or, in other words, since Israel was considered a Jewish state, all Jews or Israelites throughout the world must support that state and are loyal to it, for they are automatically citizens of Israel by virtue of their Jewishness. Consequently, all Jews must be Israelis. This reconceptualization of Jews as Israelis (and hence, as potential Nazis) is not peculiar to Germany alone, but it has been a comforting means, particularly for Germans, to express their anti-Semitic sentiments in an open way. Whether it is a conscious or unconscious anti-Semitism does not matter. What matters is that there is still a great tendency among Germans to operate on Jews as stereotypes, and this tendency has been exploited by anti-Semites to transform Jews into Nazis. This operation is typical of the new German-Jewish symbiosis put forth by Henryk Broder, one of the most outspoken critics of German anti-Semitism: it is the Germans who will never forgive the Jews for Auschwitz.[18] Their complaint could be loudly heard each time the Holocaust and anti-Semitism became a major topic for discussion during the 1970s and 1980s. Instead of working through their Judeophobia, the questions of guilt, oppression, and crimes, numerous Germans reversed the relationship of victim and victimizer and accused the Jews of causing them to suffer. The telecast of the American TV series "The Holocaust" is a case in point.

When shown in 1979, the Germans made a solemn national occasion out of it. Millions of viewers watched the series on three successive nights. It appeared that a Hollywood sentimental version of the Holocaust had more of a traumatic impact on the German nation than all the more serious educational and scholarly endeavors up to that point. Polls were taken about the reactions of the Germans to the series, their views about Jews, and their knowledge of the Nazi past. It seemed that the "TV Holocaust" had brought about a national cathartic effect and enabled Germans finally to mourn and bury the past. However, within a year or so after the initial polls had been taken, it was apparent that anti-Semitism was on the rise again and the "mourning" had not really taken place but rather a perverse shift in attitudes toward Jews and the past.[19]

Many young German writers began producing books about the suffering they and their parents underwent during the Nazi period.[20] The most notorious response to the TV Holocaust was by a left-liberal filmmaker, Edgar Reitz, who wrote and directed a TV mini-series entitled "Heimat" ("Homeland," 1984), which dealt with the period from 1918 to the present and did not show one anti-Semitic scene or Jew.[21] Rather, the major theme was the trial and tribulations of simple German folk and how they valiantly sought to maintain a sense of their true home. It was possible to view the series—and millions did—without realizing that a crucial aspect of the Nazi program was racial superiority, social engineering, and the extermination of the Jews.[22] This is not to say that Reitz was uncritical of Nazism and the material-ism of present-day Germans. Yet, the major focus of the film was on the *victimization* of the good, naïve Germans. Reitz purposely made this film in response to the "Holocaust," and in many ways, it signaled the trend toward nationalism of the 1980s, the growing insensitivity toward Jews, and the desire to rewrite history to make it clear that the Germans would never forgive the Jews for Auschwitz. Indeed, as chancellor Helmut Schmidt remarked on a return flight from Israel in 1981, "German foreign policy can and will no longer be overshadowed by Auschwitz."[23]

Three major incident of the 1980s reveal how the tables were reversed for the Jews in Germany and how the Jew in general became reconceptualized into a type of aggressor/oppressor: the Fassbinder scandal, the Bitburg affair, and the quarrel of the historians known as the *Historikerstreit*.[24]

In 1985, three years after the death of the remarkable film director and playwright Rainer Werner Fassbinder, Günter

Rühle, the intendant of the Frankfurt Kammerspiele, decided to produce Fassbinder's provocative play, *Garbage, The City and Death,* but instead created a national scandal.[25] The real play was never performed, for another kind of dramatic spectacle occurred with German Jews in the audience taking the stage while a thousand people outside the theater protested the production of the alleged anti-Semitic play by Fassbinder. Charges and counter-charges followed with Rühle, who was also the play's director, supposedly asserting that the "no hunting season for Jews was over" in West Germany. Or, in other words, Germans should feel free to make them targets of criticism, even if it meant contributing to anti-Semitic stereotypes.

Fassbinder's pathetic play, which anyone can purchase in book form, reeks with stereotypes, as does Gerhard Zwerenz's *Die Erde ist unbewohnbar wie der Mond* (*The Earth Is as Uninhabitable as the Moon*), the novel, on which it is based. The plot, if there is one, concerns the Rich Jew, who seeks revenge on Müller, a transvestite, whom he suspects of having murdered his parents during the Nazi period. Müller's wife, who is in a wheelchair, had beaten their daughter, and he himself had raped his daughter. The daughter, Roma, is a prostitute who enjoys the Rich Jew's patronage. Eventually, however, the Rich Jew murders her at her request and escapes prosecution because he is good friends with Müller II, the corrupt police chief, who appears to be at the beck and call of the Rich Jew. In fact, the Rich Jew is a super-Jew, whose effect in Germany is described rather straightforwardly and seriously in the play by another character called Hans von Gluck:

> He's sucking us dry, the Jew. Drinking our blood and blaming everything on us because he's a Jew and we're guilty. I rack my brains and I brood. I tear at my nerves. I'm going under. I wake up nights, my throat like it's a noose, death stalking me in person.

My reason tells me that they're just images, myths from the pre-history of our fathers. I feel a sharp pain on my left side. My heart, I ask myself? Or the gallbladder? And it's the Jew's fault. Just being there he makes us guilty. If he stayed where he came from or if they gassed him I'd be able to sleep better. They forgot to gas him. This is no joking matter. And I rub my hands together as I imagine him breathing his last in the gas chamber. I rub my hands together again and I moan and I rub and I say "I'm Rumpelstiltskin: ah how fine that no one knows this name is mine." He's always one step ahead and all he leaves us is charity. Garbage, worthless objects.[26]

What is interesting about this passage in the play is the representation of the Jew as the troublemaker and oppressor. He seemingly has control over Germany, the Müllers, the average Germans, who, though portrayed as demented and pathological, are subjected to his will. It is actually a moot point whether the play in its entirety is anti-Semitic. The significant feature about the play and the scandal is that Jews (in the text, on stage, and in reality) were transformed into aggressors. In fact, Jews were placed into the position of proving to the public why they shouldn't be portrayed as enormously rich and powerful, for parallels were drawn to some of the Jewish real estate magnates in Frankfurt, who ostensibly served as models for the play. As Rühle and others who supported his position implied, it was time to depict Jews as they are, to put them in their place, that is, back in their place, to be hunted. As if this had not always been the case.

Although the Fassbinder scandal was extremely controversial in West Germany, it barely attracted notice on the international scene. But another affair did, and it was very much in keeping with the perverse state of the contemporary German-Jewish symbiosis. This time, on May 5, 1985, the United States government played a role in fostering anti-Semitism in the Bitburg affair.[27] Chancellor Helmut Kohl invited President Reagan to place a wreath on an unknown soldier's grave to honor the dead Germans who had served their fatherland during World War II. The fact that there were dead SS soldiers in this cemetery and the fact that most German soldiers had fought not just for the fatherland but also to keep the concentration camps operating did not seem to bother either Kohl or Reagan, who tried to compensate for his insensitivity by honoring the dead at the former Nazi concentration camp at Bergen-Belsen during this same European trip. Both Kohl and Reagan rationalized the Bitburg event by claiming that they wanted to bury the past and honor "innocent" victims of the war. Yet, as Hajo Funke has pointed out,

> the purpose and function of this staged ceremony was not merely that of classical "defensive aggression": clearly Germany did not want to be reminded once again of the humiliation of the defeat. Consequently they tend to blame those who remind them as the ones who are guilty of the evil—in the sense of the psychoanalytic concept of projection. However, in the case of Bitburg, this defensive aggression was also linked with the attempt to redefine and re-interpret Hitler's war as a "normal" military conflict of national combatants instead of a war of aggression and genocide of inferior races (such as the Jews and, to a lesser extent, the Poles and Russians)."[28]

In short, Kohl's and Reagan's acts of normalization at Bitburg basically revealed how "unmastered" the past was, especially in Germany, where the issue about who was victimized during World War II had become clouded over by yet another affair called the Historikerstreit.

The initiator of this "quarrel of the historians" was the renowned philosopher Jürgen Habermas who, on July 11, 1986, published "Eine Art Schadensabwicklung" ("A Kind of Settlement of Damages") in the influential weekly *Die Zeit,* directed at the conservative revisionism of three prominent historians, Michael Stürmer, Ernst Nolte, and Andreas Hillgruber. Essentially, he accused all three of seeking to re-create a conventional German national identity by minimizing the devastatingly unique role that National Socialism played in the German historical development. Habermas attacked Stürmer for claiming that West Germany has assumed its rightful historical role as the centerpiece of the European defensive arc in the Atlantic system against the Red menace,[29] thereby enabling historians to interpret the significance of West Germany's relationship to the West in a more positive manner than had previously been done and also to misinterpret it. As Habermas demonstrated, this is the mistake of Andreas Hillgruber's book, *Zweierlei Untergang. Die Zerschlagung des deutschen Reichs und das Ende des europäischen Judentums (Two Kinds of Decline. The Destruction of the German Empire and the End of European Jewry),*[30] in which the historian adopts the perspective of the "brave" fighting German men and depicts the German military effort in Soviet occupied areas from 1941 to 1944 as a noble effort to hold the front so the German populace would be protected from the terrifying onslaught of Russian soldiers. (No mention is made of the fact that the prolongation of the war meant a prolongation of the concentration camps and the extermination of Jews, who were executed in mass murders as the noble German soldiers marched into the Soviet Union.) Hillgruber allegedly promotes a conservative ideological "myth" by making German soldiers into victims who fought on the right side of the war against communism. According to Habermas, such rationalization of the Nazi war effort was carried to an even greater extreme by Nolte, who subordinated Hitler's crimes to Stalin's.[31] Arguing that the concept of Nazi annihilation stemmed from a long tradition of reactions to modernization and that the Nazi exterminations were not so different from others such as those conducted under Stalin and the Pol Pot regime, Nolte maintained that the only thing unique about the Nazi program of exterminating Jews and others was the technical procedure of gassing. Since Hitler was fearful of Russian extermination, and since the Jews had by 1938 ostensibly declared war against the Germans, it can be presumed that the Nazis reacted quite "normally" to a threat. Yet, it is this very *normalization* of the Nazi past that Habermas declared dangerous and abhorrent.

For the next two years there were intense debates among prominent historians inside and outside Germany as to whether it was time to reconsider the fascist period as just another "normal" phase in German history or to keep it as a unique period that demands special attention and treatment. In an important study devoted to the entire quarrel, Charles S. Maier tended to view the debate itself as a positive sign of the development of democracy and free speech in West Germany.

> The revisionist theses may yet prove to have undermined the taboos of West Germany civic culture. If it has become acceptable to think the unthinkable (or at least to speak the hitherto unspeakable) about Auschwitz, then other debates will also open. This is not to say that only the Right will consider new options. A feeling of being victimized, a yearning for national sovereignty may lead some conservatives in the Federal Republic to weigh a West German nuclear deterrent or their own arrangement with the East. So too, the hope of a neutralized Central Europe may beckon some of the Left once again. The debate over the national past will have served to licence a debate over the German future.[32]

Those remarks, written in 1988, were prematurely optimistic. The quarrel never took root in German society as a whole, for it never led to the growth of an open discourse about the Holocaust, anti-Semitism, and German responsibility. Habermas and his supporters were left marginalized, as Germans rushed to reunification in another step to bury the Nazi past. The "quarrel" did not indicate how "democratic" Germany had become so that the most taboo subject imaginable could be debated in the public arena. Rather, it was another sanitation measure to cleanse Germany's image as a model state for the 1990s. The quarrel blurred moral categories; it did not clarify them. If it had any social and political meaning, the *Historikerstreit* signaled how German nationalism had become respectable again and how it had legitimated itself by showing how Germans had been wronged and victimized during the "normal" period of fascism.

The quarrel of the historians, the Fassbinder scandal, and the Bitburg affair contributed to the growing fear, held by Jews living in Germany, that anti-Semitism might soon return in a violent form. In fact, as in France and other countries, there has been an increase of damage done to Jewish cemeteries and public buildings, not to mention widespread anti-Semitic graffiti, the increased activity of extreme right parties, more neo-fascist publications slandering Jews and "exposing the lie" of the Holocaust.[33] However, instead of trying to remain anonymous, as most German Jews did up to the end of the 1970s, there has been a more active response on the part of individual Jews and the Jewish communities. Until the Fassbinder affair of 1985, the German Jews had been politically divided in their response to anti-Semitism, the German government's policies, and Israel. To a great extent, this division had a great deal to do with age and socialization. The older Jews, who had survived the Nazi genocide and who had largely come from Eastern European countries, had constantly made compromises with the German philo-Semitic policies and felt protected by the government. Moreover, they were staunch supporters of Israel, and as long as the government provided reparations and backed Israel, they did not want to rock the boat. Their major concern was safety and freedom to pursue their religious beliefs and professional interests. They kept to themselves, or, if they were assimilated, they kept their "Jewishness" to themselves.

On the other hand, there are two younger generations of Jews living in Germany today, and they tend to be less willing to make compromises with the German government or with German anti-Semitism. Most of these German Jews went through the German educational system, and if identified as Jews, they experienced a healthy dose of anti-Semitism that offset the official philo-Semitism of the government. Moreover, they felt shame and anxiety at home because of their parents' silence and fears. However, almost all these younger Jews were involved in Zionist activities, visited Israel often, and came to identify with Israel in a positive sense. That is, the state of Israel embodied part of their identity and gave them the courage to speak out, as independent Jews, who did not have to fear calling themselves Jews, no matter what kind of Jew they were. Therefore, many of the first generation of young Jews (born between 1945–55) participated in the student movement of the 1960s and began attacking the German government and the United States. To make the matter even more complicated, they began to have doubts about the policies of Israel. This is not to say that all of the younger German Jews were on the Left. The majority were probably more liberal than their parents, but not really radical. However, whether radical or liberal, the quandary for these younger Jews and their children was a growing split in their loyalties and identities because, at the onset of the 1970s, they began criticizing their parents and the German government for hypocritical politics that supported racism and imperialism *and* the student movement for its anti-Semitism that posed as anti-Zionism. In addition to this quandary, there was a greater tendency toward assimilation and intermarriage in West Germany so that many of the young Jews found themselves speaking out and claiming their Jewish identity while turning atheist, or reclaiming their Jewish identity to spite anti-Semitism of all kinds.

By the time of the Fassbinder affair, the divisions among older and younger Jews had grown considerably in West Germany, and if this 1985 controversy had any positive effect, it was the solidarity shown by the Frankfurt Jewish community, where believers and non-believers, young and old, right and left, took a public stand together against anti-Semitism. This public stance was one of the first expressions of such solidarity. It opened the way, especially for the second generation of young German Jews, to speak out about Jewish issues, whether to criticize anti-Semitism in West Germany, Jewish corruption in West Germany, or the oppression of Palestinians in Israel. Several journals and magazines, such as *Babylon,* were founded to offset the more conservative Jewish voices in Germany and to provide a more differentiated picture of who the Jews are and what their religion, culture, and politics are.

Of course, the Jews are changing in reunified Germany today. Thousands of Soviet Jews have arrived and may continue to arrive. Israelis have settled down in Germany. The older East European generation is disappearing. The politics of the official Jewish communities have become more critical of the German government as the Federal Republic has become more nationalist and more pro Arab. The biggest change of all since the reunification is symbolized, I believe, by the tearing down of the Berlin Wall on November 9, 1989, the date on which the infamous Jewish pogrom of 1938, *Kristallnacht* or Crystal Night, had generally been commemorated in West Germany. For the Germans this was a proud day of rebirth, while that rebirth was also a day of mourning for the Jews. It is a day that Germans will never want to forget because it symbolized their reunion, but in order not to forget it, they must forget Crystal Night. German history must be "normalized" by eliminating the Holocaust. Once again, there must be an operation that will change Jews and Germans and that will be reinforced by the new anti-Semitism, which is taking hold not only in Germany but also in the United States and other parts of the world.

Perhaps the most incisive analysis of how the operation on Jews has led to a new kind of anti-Semitism is the brilliant and meticulous work of the French scholar Pierre André Taguieff.[34] Based on his exhaustive research on anti-Semitic acts, publications, documents, and tendencies mainly in France, Taguieff's work is highly significant because his conclusions have parallels throughout the world. Put another way, if France harbors a new form of anti-Semitism, then one can expect operations to be performed on Jews throughout the world, for France is generally considered a modern state distinguished by its tolerant attitude toward Jews and support of Israel. Yet, somehow it is normal, even after the Holocaust, to be tolerant and threatening toward Jews at the same time. It is this disturbing condition, the normalization of a very complex and insidious form of anti-Semitism, that Taguieff seeks to expose.

For Taguieff, two conditions have been necessary for anti-Semitism to have become legitimate, acceptable, and honorable during the past thirty years: 1) anti-Jewish discourse had to be retranslated into an anti-Zionist discourse; 2) Zionism had to be reinterpreted as a repulsive myth and associated with imperialism. These two factors have allowed national revolutionary movements, whether it be in Africa or the Middle East, to disassociate the nationalism of Israel from a political-ethical standpoint so that Zionism itself is regarded as a form of racism and imperialism. Therefore, the fight against Israel is a struggle against imperialism and racism. In addition to this proposition is the *essentialist* argument (never openly asserted) that all Jews are Zionists, actually or virtually, admittedly or shamefully. That is, their common nature compels them to be Zionists. The Jew is essentially Zionist, thus racist, no matter what he or she may think, or do (3).

According to Taguieff, this new anti-Semitic synthesis, which has led to a new "conceptual Jew," was prepared during the 1950s (somewhat underground but seeping every now and then into the public arena) and "blossomed" between 1967 and 1975. There are two distinguishable tendencies on the Right and on the Left that formed the synthesis, although both have made use of the traditional religious and racial prejudices against Jews.

During the period in question, neo-fascist publications and organizations sought to negate the existence of gas chambers and to question the truth of the genocide. Since Jews allegedly control the mass media and banks, they argued, the Jews could create and perpetuate the lie of the Holocaust. In other words, there has been a Jewish conspiracy against truth, which writers like Robert Faurisson, who has his followers throughout the world, have sought to uncover. As soon as Jews enter into a debate with Faurisson and his supporters, they are in a double bind, for their willingness to debate with him is an admission that there may be some truth to his argument, and their rejection can be read as an effort to conceal the true facts. The real carriers of the truth are the oppressed and victims, i.e. former Nazis and neo-Nazis. The revision of history has led to a central image: Israel and the Diaspora constitute a "Jewish International" (the Zionist International) which seeks the domination of the world and draws its legitimacy by pretending to have been victimized during World War II.

On the Left of the political spectrum, the Communist Party and the radicals in support of the Palestinian Liberation movement began cultivating their anti-Jewish myth from a basic hatred of conquerors and a critique of imperialism. Israel, supported by the United States, revealed its true colors in 1967 and began expanding and colonizing Arab territories. As colonialists and imperialists, the Israelis treated the Arabs in a racist and oppressive manner, and since all Jews throughout the world allegedly support Israel, Judaism itself was identified with Zionism, which was equated with imperialism and an international Jewish conspiracy.

Taguieff maintains that there was a reinscription of the anti-Semitic discourse into the neo-fascist discourse in France by 1975. It was comprised by the following: a) Judaism and Zionism do not differ in any manner; b) Zionism, that is Judaism, is fundamentally racist; c) therefore, anti-Zionism, which is confused with anti-Judaism, is a form of anti-racism (17).

As I have pointed out before in a different context, one of the weird outcomes of this line of argumentation has been to "nazify" the Jews. If to be a Jew is to be a racist, then all Jews are potentially Nazis (Zionism = racism = Nazism). This equation was eventually proved for many by the Jewish involvement in the massacres of Sabra and Schatilla, i.e. the Jews want to massacre and exterminate the Palestinians and Arabs, whose true home has been invaded by a "cancerous growth."

This new way of conceptualizing Jews will make it extremely difficult to combat anti-Semitism and to stop anti-Semitic operations, for the new Judeophobia functions with or without racism, but also with or without anti-racism. As Taguieff points out, anti-Semitism can no longer be reduced to a biological or cultural form of racism, and the fact that anti-Semitism cannot be derived from racism has its first logical consequence: we cannot link together the struggle against racism with the struggle against anti-Semitism. On the contrary, the struggle against racism, despite our human desires for unity, has had to submit to a cleavage, for it masks exigencies that are sometimes contradictory.

For instance, it happens at times that, in order to combat the new anti-Semitism, one must fight against this or that form of anti-racism (44).

> Since there is no longer any significant correlation between racism and anti-Semitism, we have entered an era of post-anti-Semitism in a strict sense. To be precise, we are the observers in a period of transition in which discourses are being confused and in which anti-Jewish racism continues to interfere with the anti-Jewish anti-racism that has emerged. It is also possible to propose the following interpretation: the period of ideological transformation in which we are living is one of the convergence of the old and new traditions of anti-Jewish discourse: racial anti-Semitism and anti-racist anti-Zionism, political anti-Semitism and negative revisionism of history, popular/populist Catholic anti-Semitism, and progressive anti-Semitism that denounces Zionism as racism. (45)

Given these new conditions of anti-Semitism, Taguieff believes that "Jews are caught in a double bind, for they can only displease their critics and others by what they do. They can only act within the constraints placed on them. In other words, they can only incorporate one or the other of the two principle figures established by their adversaries: to become ethno-centered and nationalist, or to defend the memory of Shoah, which is branded a lie" (45).

As I remarked before, Taguieff's analysis is especially important because it can be applied to the dilemma of Jews throughout the world and sheds light on the concept of the operated Jew, a concept that should not be misunderstood as implying that Jews are passive bodies and simply allow themselves to be operated on. What I want to suggest by this image is that there is a fusion of the social engineering of modernism, the reification process of late capitalism, and traditional forms of anti-Semitism that sets the context for the way outsiders define Jews and the way Jews define themselves. The overall mode of definition has a great deal to do with *daily* stigmatization, endowing Jews with dangerous genetic diseases and/or demonic capacities, as Dietz Bering has demonstrated in his very important book, *Der Name als Stigma;*[35] the stigmatization is related to the question of power and the way Jews are operated on by the dominant/dominating outside world and bodies, operate on one another, and operate on themselves in an almost desperate endeavor to achieve an autonomous Jewish identity that will simultaneously function as an acceptable part of the larger body to which they belong. The operated Jew is always active, changing, trying on new bodies, if you will, new parts, to fit into the scheme of perfecting the world and to become part of the world's operations. Nothing has made this clearer to me than Paul Breines's illuminating book *Tough Jews.*[36]

Published in 1990 but written over the course of the past eight years, Breines' book is both a passionate critique of American Jewry and its obsession with becoming tough *and* an urgent plea to resist gently those forces of "Zionization" and "Americanization" that have brought out the "fascist" potential of American Jews and Israelis alike. As he states,

> the Trauma of Nazi mass murder made the Jewish yearning for toughness especially strong, while nearly two thousand years of self-definition according to an ethos of meekness and gentleness made toughness unacceptable. Unwilling to reject either fully, the Israeli and the post-Holocaust American Jew have sought to have *both.* They want in Israel, a moral *Machtstaat,* a conqueror state with a conscience; they want to subordinate others or to kill while themselves remaining the chosen people, "a light unto the nations." (18)

Breines is disturbed by the fact that the images of the Jewish victim and of the Holocaust are used by Jews to rationalize the manner in which Jews victimize others, particularly the Palestinians. Throughout his book he discusses various aspects of the body, and how Jews, who have been stereotyped as gentle and meek, have longed for another type of a muscular and tough body. In this respect, Israel is the embodiment of a Jewish fantasy, but a perverted one. As he notes,

> it may be that the notion of the primacy of ethics in Jewish life and of the Jew as uniquely ethical or gentle was a function of the history of Jewish exclusion from the world of bodies (material production, conquest, combat). The experience of many Jews in the United States and Israel indicates an erosion of that notion as Jewish participation in the world of bodies increases. With grim irony, Zionism's vision of a normalized Jewry has in part been *realized* in Israeli brutality toward Palestinians, for in the framework of civilized nations, brutality is the very essence of normalcy. It was their statelessness, defenselessness, and gentleness, after all, that had made Jews eccentric. (50)

While I agree with Breines's critique of "Jewish" normalization, that is, the transformation of American and Israeli Jews into tough Jews, I think the focus of the critique is somewhat blurred and askew. Perhaps I am misreading him, for he appears to hold American Jews and Israelis responsible for their fantasies, self-images, and images and expects them through their actions to project a rejuvenated image of the gentle but firm Jew. Such an expectation, however, is dependent on the rational choice theory which purports that individuals can methodologically, through choices and actions or through their wills, determine their identities and images. There are many fallacies to this theory because it does not take into account factors of space, place, and history in a differentiated world. In the case of Jews, the most important factor to be taken into consideration is the shifting but constant manipulation of the Jewish image by outside forces and the stigmatization associated with the definition of the Jew, whether the definition is made by Jew or non-Jew. Though Breines often touches on the problem of manipulation and operation, he loses sight of the combination of forces that gave rise to the tough Jew because he himself wants to assume a "new" Jewish body that exposes the old one for its racism while fending off charges of Jewish self-hate by taking pride in Jewish eccentricity and marginality.

What was fascinating to me in reading Breines's book was the sense he conveyed of the operations that he had undergone while writing it, that is, his own sensitive operations and transformations. At one point he states that he began his study as an "insistent partisan" of the view that the real Jew was always gentle and that the tough Jew is not really Jewish. "Israeli behavior toward Palestinians and American Jewish fantasies about that behavior, for example, seemed to me not merely cruel and stupid, but fundamentally un-Jewish. I can no longer agree with that last point" (29). Breines consulted with numerous friends and colleagues during the writing of his very personal book from 1982 to 1989, beginning with the Israeli invasion of Lebanon and ending, I assume, sometime after the tearing down of the Berlin Wall and the increased violence in the Israeli occupied territories. He rewrote the book, as he claims, several times, and one can gain a sense of his shifting positions during the past seven years on his own Jewishness and the prescribed images and self-designed images of Jews. In fact, there is something "unique" in Breines's writing and thought processes that reflects upon the unique condition of the operated Jew in the 20th century: Breines writes and thinks of strategies to define Jews so that something essential to the Jewish *tradition* will not be extinguished, or he writes himself into the body of the Jewish tradition with the hope that neither he nor the gentle ethics will be exterminated. Put another way, he wants to revive a part of the Jewish body that is malfunctioning, and this malfunctioning is tied to nationalism and Zionism/Americanism (code words, I believe, for the reification process and male domination in late capitalism). Breines wants American Jews and Israelis to resist the operation of normalization that has transformed a good many of them into brutal nationalists and Zionists. Jews are to remain the Other, to reside on borders and margins, to keep on the move, perhaps so they will not be an easy target, and yet, they are to set themselves up as the ideal targets of gentleness.

It is Breines's own resisting and resistance as an alternative to normalization in American and Israeli life that point to the crucial theme of his book: the social engineering and instrumental reason in Western society that foster, censor, curb, and maintain images and self-images of Jews. Normalization of Jews in the post-Holocaust world was a necessity if anti-Semitism was to be maintained in a *new* political form. Though it may be true that there were always "tough Jews" in Jewish history and that Jews always had the potential to become "normally" brutal, it is also true that they came to serve a unique symbol in modern society for all those diseased and dangerous elements that had to be eliminated. Therefore, the establishment of the state of Israel as a Jewish body would not have come about if it were not going to continue to serve a purpose, which Jews themselves help to generate and propel. The Jewish body/state *normalizes* anti-Semitism and racism by distracting us from the real diseases and dangers in the world, and if viewed as a "cancerous growth," it must eventually be eliminated, simply because no amount of operations will save it. In this way, both Jews and Arabs can be blamed for a sick situation and be pitted against one another as two hopelessly diseased bodies. Only the surgical knife of the civilized Westerners can restore the world order, or better yet, create a clean New World Order.

What is unique about the situation of the Jews in the twentieth century is that there is no ethnic group or culture still faced with the question of real extinction, for *normalization,* whether it be in the West or the Middle East, has meant for Jews changing oneself to fit in, become anonymous, or more nationalistic than the so-called natives of a nation with the expectation that whatever is Jewish about one's identity will eventually be made extinct or will be eliminated. It is also true that, for most minority groups in the modern nation-states of the West, normalization probably means discarding one's heritage and cultural identity. But again, the operations that the Jews have been called upon to perform and to undergo are unique if not grotesque because, ultimately, Jews under various names and forms are conjured and conceived to be destroyed or to destroy themselves.

Such a pessimistic conclusion is not my conclusion, but it does lead me back to the grotesque stories of Panizza and Friedlaender, and to the reasons why I have felt urged to publish their stories. Like Zygmunt Bauman, I believe that until the unique aspects of the Holocaust are historically and personally grasped so that they become part of our normative behavior, we shall continue to perpetuate the conditions that enable us to kill and murder inimical agents and dangerous people with a clean conscience and in the name of civilization against barbarism. I am not convinced that rational argument and persuasion can make us return to the past to understand why we have reached our present state of dangerous, calculating behavior. That is why I have chosen haunting and macabre images of the past with the hope that they might jar us out of our present detachment.

Operated Jews and operated goys are not just indicative of the distorted relations between Jews and gentiles. The German-

Jewish symbiosis is not a problem just for Germans and Jews. The Holocaust is not just the outcome of German anti-Semitism. The Arab endeavors to drive the Israelis into the ocean and the oppressive treatment of the Palestinians by Israelis are not just an extension of German history or the German-Jewish symbiosis. We are all involved and continue to be responsible for racism, anti-Semitism, and war. Unique as all these problems and distant as some of the events may be, they are common factors in a civilizing process that has hardened us against the outrages performed in its name. As Theodor Adorno and Max Horkheimer wrote in *Dialectic of Enlightenment,* "the hardened individual represents that which is better only in relation in a hardened society, and not in absolute terms. He reflects the shame felt at everything the collective system inflicts on the individual and what happens when there are no more individuals."[37]

These words were written in 1944 by two German-Jewish intellectuals living in American exile about the common tendencies they saw in German fascism and American liberal capitalism.

Notes

1. In 1991, the situation changed when the Iraqis used Scud missiles to attack Israel and when the Palestinians supported these attacks. The discord among Jews was transformed into international solidarity. However, this fragile solidarity may eventually collapse now that the war in the Persian Gulf has come to an end.

2. *Illuminations,* trs. Harry Zohn (New York: Harcourt, Brace & World, 1968), 257. Benjamin repeatedly revised and elaborated his notion of the dialectical image in stillstand toward the end of his life. See also the chapter entitled "N: Erkenntnistheoretisches, Theories des Fortshritts" in Walter Benjamin, *Das Passagen-Werk,* ed. Rolf Tiedemann, vol. I (Frankfurt am Main: Suhrkamp, 1983), 570–611. "In the dialectical

image the past of a certain epoch is always simultaneously the 'has—been-like-that.' However, it only appears as such to a very specific epoch: the one in which humankind, rubbing its eyes, recognizes this dream image as such. It is in this moment that the historian assumes the task of dream interpretation" (580).

3. *Modernity and the Holocaust* (Ithaca: Cornell University Press, 1989).

4. Bauman, *Modernity and the Holocaust,* 65.

5. See Martin Gilbert, *Auschwitz and the Allies* (London: M. Joseph/Rainbird, 1981); Michael R. Marrus, *The Unwanted: European Refugees in the Twentieth Century* (New York: Oxford University Press, 1985); Monty Noam Penkower, *The Jews Were Expendable: Free World Diplomacy and the Holocaust* (Urbana: University of Illinois Press, 1983); and David S. Wyman, *The Abandonment of the Jews: America and the Holocaust, 1941–1945* (New York: Pantheon, 1984).

6. In his perceptive essay on this subject, "Is Anti-Zionism a New Form of Antisemitism?" in *Antisemitism in the Contemporary World,* ed. Michael Curtis (Boulder: Westview Press, 1986), 145–54, Dan V. Segre uses the same metaphor. "The recurring feature of this Manichean phenomenon among those who view Zionism as political, social, and religious satanism is the polarization, accumulation, and worldwide extension of the negative perception of the Jewish national movement. By *polarization* I mean the lack of gradualism in the hostility toward Zionism. For those who oppose it, Zionism is not a bad political phenomenon; it is a cancerous growth, a monster" (145).

7. See Sander L. Gilman, *Difference and Pathology: Stereotypes of Sexuality, Race and Madness* (Ithaca: Cornell University Press, 1985).

8. In 1980 and 1981, three special issues of *New German Critique* were devoted to this topic, and many of the essays in those issues along with new ones were eventually published as a book. See Anson Rabinbach and Jack Zipes, eds., *Germans and Jews since the Holocaust: The Changing Situation in West Germany* (New York: Holmes & Meier, 1986). See also the recent studies in Germany: Micha Brumlik, Doron Kiesel, Cilly Kugelmann, Julius H. Schoeps, eds., *Jüdisches Leben in Deutschland seit 1945* (Frankfurt am Main: Athenäum, 1986), Günter Gorschenek and Stephan Reimers, eds. *Offene Wunden—brennende Fragen: Juden in Deutschland von 1938 bis heute* (Frankfurt am Main: Josef Knecht,

1989), and Michael Wolffsohn, *Ewige Schuld? 40 Jahre Deutsch-Jüdisch-Israelische Beziehungen* (Munich: Piper, 1988).

9. "Against the Myth of the German-Jewish Dialogue," in *On Jews and Judaism: Selected Essays* (New York: Schocken, 1976), 63.

10. For an excellent summary of this debate with regard to the present situation in Germany, see Anson Rabinbach, "Reflections on Germans and Jews since Auschwitz," in *Germans and Jews since the Holocaust: The Changing Situation in West Germany* (New York: Holmes & Meier, 1986), 3–24.

11. "Negative Symbiose," *Babylon* 1 (1986), 9.

12. For a superb treatment of this period in German history, see Frank Stern, *The Whitewashing of the Yellow Badge: Antisemitism and Philosemitism in West Germany 1945–1952* (University of Tel Aviv, PhD Dissertation, 1988) and "The Historic Triangle: Occupiers, Germans and Jews in Postwar Germany," in *Tel Aviver Jahrbuch für deutsche Geschichte* 19 (1990), 47–76.

13. There are very few documents about Jews in East Germany, but recently some important studies have appeared. See Lothar Mertens, "Juden in der DDR: Eine schwindende Minderheit," *Deutschland Archiv* 19 (November 1986), 1192–1203, and Siegfried Theodor Arndt, Helmut Eschwege, Peter Honigmann, and Lothar Mertens, *Juden in der DDR, Geschichte—Probleme—Perspektive* (Cologne: Universität Gesamthochschule Duisburg, 1988).

14. See his remarks in his autobiographical essay in Hans Jürgen Schultz, *Mein Judentum* (Stuttgart: Kreuz Verlag, 1978), 15. In his critique of Israeli politics, Becker equates Jews with Israelis, whom he calls "Herrenmenschen," a term associated with Nazis.

15. During the political changes of 1989–90, the fact that several prominent reformers like Klaus Gysi were of Jewish background was made into a problem for them since they were not considered "German."

16. See Andrei S. Markovits, "Germans and Jews: The Continuation of an Uneasy Relationship," *Jewish Frontier* 543 (April 1984), 14–20.

17. Jacob Alson, Benjamin R. Epstein, and Nathan C. Belth, "Germany Nine Years Later: A Report of the Anti-Defamation League of B'nai B'rith of a Study Tour Undertaken at the Invitation of the Federal Republic of West Germany," unpublished (July 1954), 12–13. Italics are mine.

18. See Henryk M. Broder, *Der Ewige AntiSemit: Über Sinn und Funktion eines beständigen Gefühls* (Frankfurt am Main: Fischer, 1986), 125–164.

19. See Peter Märthesheimer and Ivo Frenzel, eds., *Im Kreuzfeuer: Der Fernsehfilm 'Holocaust'* (Frankfurt: Fischer, 1979) and Friedrich Knilli and Siegfried Zielinski, eds., *Holocaust zur Unterhaltung: Anatomie eines internationalen Bestsellers* (Berlin: Elefanten Press, 1982).

20. See Michael Schneider, "Fathers and Sons, Retrospectively: The Damaged Relationship Between Two Generations," *New German Critique* 31 (Winter 1984), 3–52. Originally published in German in Schneider's book, *Den Kopf verkehrt aufgesetzt* (Darmstadt: Luchterhand, 1981).

21. See Bruce Murray, "National Socialism, Docudramas, and the Development of Public Opinion: A Contrastive Analysis of 'Holocaust' and 'Heimat'," *Germanistische Medienwissenschaft*, Eds. Friedrich Knilli and Siegfried Zielinski (Bern: Peter Lang, 1989), 89–109.

22. See Miriam Hansen, "Dossier on *Heimat*," *New German Critique* 36 (Fall 1985), 3–24. See especially the remarks by Gertrud Koch, "How Much Naïveté Can We Afford? The New *Heimat* Feeling": "Reitz actually puts his finger on the problem, i.e., that in order to tell the myth of "*Heimat*" the trauma of Auschwitz has to be bracketed from German history. Thus Reitz has to revise history—but can one do so in a naïve way? Unmistakably, *Heimat* coincides with a political climate which is distinguished by certain semantic slippages, from Auschwitz over Stalingrad into Hunsrück, by a shift in the paradigms of historical interpretation from 'everyday fascism' to 'fascist' everday life" (13–14).

23. Cited in Wolffsohn in *Ewige Schuld?*, 42.

24. Cf. Anson Rabinbach, "The Jewish Question in the German Question," *New German Critique* 44 (Spring/Summer, 1988), 159–92, and Moishe Postone, "After the Holocaust: History and Identity in West Germany," in *Coping with the Past: Germany and Austria after 1945*, ed. Kathy Harms, L. R. Reuter, and V. Dürr (Madison: University of Wisconsin Press, 1991), 233–51.

25. See Andrei S. Markovits, Seyla Benhabib, Moishe Postone, "Symposium on Rainer Werner Fassbinder's *Garbage, the City and Death*," *New German Critique* 38 (Spring/Summer 1986), 3–27, and Sigrid Meuschel, "The Search for 'Normality' in the Relationship between Germans and Jews," *New German Critique* 38 (Spring/Summer 1986), 39–56.

26. Rainer Werner Fassbinder, *Plays,* trans. and ed., Denis Calandra (New York: PAJ Publications, 1985), 180–81.

27. See Geffrey Hartman, ed. *Bitburg in Moral and Political Perspective* (Bloomington: Indiana UP, 1986) and Ilya Levkov, *Bitburg and Beyond: Encounters in American, German and Jewish History* (New York: Shapolsky, 1987).

28. "Bitburg, Jews, and Germans: A Case Study of Anti-Jewish Sentiment in Germany during May, 1985," *New German Critique* (Spring/Summer 1986), 68.

29. See Michael Stürmer, "Suche nach der verlorenen Erinnerung," *Das Parlement* 17 (May 24, 1986), 1.

30. Berlin: Corso bei Siedler, 1986.

31. See "Between Myth and Revisionism? The Third Reich in the Perspective of the 1980s," in *Aspects of the Third Reich,* ed. H. W. Koch (London: Macmillan, 1985): 17–38, and "Vergangenheit, die nicht vergehen will," *Frankfurter Allgemeine Zeitung* (June 6, 1986).

32. *The Unmasterable Past: History, Holocaust and German National Identity* (Cambridge: Harvard University Press, 1988): 2–3.

33. On February 12, 1990 a rally was held in Leipzig during which people were urged by the NPD to invite people to attend a lecture by the British revisionist Historian David Irving and to back their demand "Germany for the Germans." At the rally some 2,000 copies of the reactionary periodical *Nation Europa* were passed out. In this special issue one could read an article entitled "The Legend of the Six Million," in which a former SS officer denied the existence of mass extermination camps. See *Blick nach Rechts* (April 9, 1990).

34. See "La nouvelle Judéophobie: Antisionisme, Antiracisme, Anti-imperialisme," *Les Temps Modernes* 520 (November, 1989), 1–80. Subsequent citations are given in the text.

35. *Der Name als Stigma: Antisemitismus im deutschen Alltag 1812–1933* (Stuttgart: Klett-Cotta, 1988).

36. *Tough Jews: Political Fantasies and the Moral Dilemma of American Jewry* (New York: Basic Books, 1990). Subsequent citations are given in the text.

37. *Dialectic of Enlightenment,* Trs. John Cumming (New York: Seabury, 1972), 242.

The Operated Jew (1893)

𝕹obody will blame me for wanting to erect a monument in honor of my friend Itzig Faitel Stern. At least, as long as this lies within my power. I almost fear that I lack such power, for Itzig Faitel Stern, my best friend at the university, was a phenomenon. It would take a linguist, a choreographer, an aesthete, an anatomist, a tailor, and a psychiatrist all in one to grasp and fully explain Faitel's entire appearance, what he said, how he walked, and what he did. Thus, it will not be surprising after what I have just said, when my sketch presents only bits and pieces. I must rely on my five senses which, according to today's prevailing school of literature, should completely suffice for creating a work of art—without attempting to ask much about the why and how and without attempting to provide artificial motivation and superficial construction. If a comedy should originate instead of a work of art, then let the school of literature bear the responsibility.

Itzig Faitel was a small, squat man. His right shoulder was

slightly higher than his left, and he had a sharp protruding chicken breast upon which he always wore a wide heavy silk tie ornamented by a dull ruby and attached to a breast-plate. The lapels on both sides of this tie ran top right to bottom left so that when Faitel moved along the curbstones, it appeared as though he were veering down the sidewalk to the other side or going in a diagonal direction. Faitel could not be convinced that the arrangement of his clothes came from the rhombic shift of his chest cage. This is why he complained terribly about Christian tailors. After all, the suits which he wore were always made from the finest worsted.

Itzig Faitel's countenance was most interesting. It is a shame that Lavater had not laid eyes upon it. An antelope's eye with a subdued, cherry-like glow swam in wide apertures of the smooth velvet, slightly yellow skin of his temple and cheeks. Itzig's nose assumed a form which was similar to that of the high priest who was the most prominent and striking figure of Kaulbach's painting "The Destruction of Jerusalem." To be sure, the eyebrows had meshed, but Faitel Stern assured me that this meshing had become very popular. He even knew that people with such eyebrows had allegedly been drowned at one time. Yet, he countered this by assuring me that he never went near water. His lips were fleshy and overly creased; his teeth sparkled like pure crystal. A violet fatty tongue often thrust itself between them at the wrong time. Neither beard nor mustache adorned the chin and upper lip, for Faitel Stern was still very young. If I may also add that my friend's lower torso had bow-legs whose angular swing was not excessive, then I believe that I have sketched Itzig's figure to a certain degree. Later I'll talk about the curly, thick black locks of hair on his head.

This, then, was the student Stern as still-life. But who will help me—what clown, what imitator of dialects, what mime—in my endeavor to depict Itzig in motion as he spoke and acted? Itzig told me that he came from a French family and was raised according to French tradition. He even spoke some French. Naturally, it was warped. It was his misfortune to have moved at a young age to the nearby Palatinate where he sucked up the enunciated sounds of this region as though they were milk and honey. Of course, Faitel could speak high German, yet it was not his language but that of a dressy doll. When Faitel was in private company and did not have to feel embarrassed, he spoke the dialects of the Palatinate—and something more than that.

Yet, before I get to this, let me make a few remarks about his way of walking and gesticulating. —When he walked, Itzig always raised both thighs almost to his midriff so that he bore some resemblance to a stork. At the same time, he lowered his head deeply into his breast-plated tie and stared at the ground. One had to assume that he could not gauge the strength needed for lifting his legs as he went head over heels. —Similar disturbances can be noted in people with spinal diseases. However, Itzig did not have a spinal disease, for he was young and in good condition. When I asked him one time why he walked so extravagantly, he said, "So I can moof ahead!" —Faitel also had trouble keeping his balance, and when he walked, there were often beads of sweat streaming from the curly locks of hair around his temple. The collar wrapped around my friend's neck was fastened tightly and firmly. I assume that this was due to the difficulty and work Itzig needed to keep his head pointed upright toward God's heavens. In its natural position, Itzig's head was always pointed toward earth, the chin drilled solidly into the silk breast-plated tie.

Such was Itzig Faitel Stern as still-life and in motion. But what were his gestures like?

Of course, this depended on Faitel's mood, whether he was disposed or indisposed; whether he was pleasant or contrary. He was never highly emotional. His constitution prevented him from getting angry. But when he became zealous and had a good opportunity to wage an argument, then he reared up, raised a hand, pulled back his fleshy, volatile upper lip like a piece of leather so that the upper row of teeth became exposed, spread open both his hands like fans pointing upward with his upper body leaning backward, bobbed his head up and down against his breast a few times, and rhythmically uttered sounds like a trumpet. Up to this moment my friend may not have said a thing. But I always knew from the entire series of gestures and expressions in what direction Faitel's arguments would move. Faitel meowed, rattled, bleated and also liked to produce sneezing sounds and at the right time so that one could infer even more from all this noise than mere words interjected here and there. If his position were dubious or even endangered, or if he wanted to convince his opponent about an impossible matter, then he threw his rotating upper body with pinched-in stomach away from the side of his opponent and toward himself as though he wanted to pull the concerned person over toward his entire corporeal mass of flesh. The burring sounds that accompanied this act were filled with zeal, grunts, and comfort. Anyone who chanced to see and hear all this for the first time would be astonished and overwhelmed. One would surrender in the debate, just in recognition of the zealous way in which he went about convincing the opponent. In realizing the effect he had, Faitel would often be driven to even greater heights. Ultimately, he would become monstrous.

So much for his agitations.

But who will help me describe Itzig Faitel Stern's speech? What philologist or expert in dialects would dare analyze this mixture of Palatinate Semitic babble, French nasal noises, and some high German vocal sounds that he had fortuitously overheard and articulated with an open position of the mouth? I can't do this. So I want to confine myself to presenting to the reader what I remember about Itzig Faitel's phrases according to the standard phonetic system. But before I do this, I must emphasize two points about Faitel's speech that are of particular grammatical interest. After this, I shall unfold the horrifying comedy, which Itzig Faitel Stern produced in Heidelberg, where we both studied, without interruption. Among the numerous and hardly perceptible peculiarities of his manner of speech, Faitel had two in particular—what I shall call speech particles—which recurred time and again and struck me finally as syntactical components of some conceptual value. Faitel Stern said something like this when I questioned him about the immense luxury of his wardrobe and toilet articles: "Why shoodn't I buy for me a new coat, a bootiful hat—menerá, fine wanished boots—menerá, me, too, I shood bicome a fine gentilman after this Deradáng! Deradáng!" His upper body rocked back and forth. At the same time, there was a spreading of the hands at shoulder height in a slightly squat position; an ecstatic look with a glossy reflection; an exposure of both rows of teeth; a rich amount of saliva.

The reader will have discovered two surprising words here, or rather an annexation, an appendage, and an interjection which cannot be found in any dictionary. "Menerá," a kind of purring word, short-long, with the stress on the last syllable (anapest), was appended with substantives, which were endowed with a consonant. Then "emenerá" was frequently added, but with such dazzling speed that the stress remained on the substantive, allowing the annex to attach itself as a purring sound with four short syllables. Many times it also seemed as if "menerá" was only to serve as the connection to the next word if the latter began with a sound that caused difficulty for Faitel's tongue. Therefore, it was only used when he talked rapidly or was in an excited mood. The two annexes lacked a declinatory character as is the case with some Negro languages. —The situation was completely different with the strongly nasal "Deradáng!" This was an interjection, an exclamatory particle. It had its own word and concept. It was sing-song, babbled with saliva in the mouth. It closed the sentence and seemed to mean so much as "Well, I'm right, aren't I?" —"You see!" —"Who would have thought of that?" —"That takes care of that!" —Yes, dear reader, try as you might to pronounce "Deradáng! Deradáng!" you will never be able to do it with such a fatty guttural noise, such soft bawling, such a great amount of spit as Itzig Faitel Stern.

Now, I no longer want to keep the reader in the dark as to how I became associated with this remarkable figure. Nor do I want to cloak my purposes in mystery and mislead the reader who might suppose that it was pity which moved me to make the close acquaintance with this dreadful piece of human flesh named Itzig Faitel Stern. There was certainly a great deal of what I would call medical or rather anthropological curiosity in this case. I was attracted to him in the same way I might be to a Negro whose goggle eyes, yellow connective optical membranes, crushed nose, mollusk lips and ivory teeth and smell one perceives altogether in wonderment and whose feelings and most secret anthropological actions one wants to get to know as well! Perhaps there was also some pity here, but not much. I observed with astonishment how this monster took terrible pains to adapt to our circumstances, our way of walking, thinking, our gesticulations, the expressions of our intellectual tradition, our manner of speech. But there was a much stronger and more egotistical reason for me since I wanted to learn something about the Talmud, which was Faitel's religious book. All the remarkable rumors spread about this vast prayer book interested me a great deal. To be sure, Itzig was not a Talmudic scholar, but he knew a great deal about the Talmud. He knew a lot of little customs, weaknesses, practices, and eccentricities, which could not be found in books and translations of the Talmud, and which had great anthropological value for me.

Of course, many of the strangest rumors were spread about

me by the students in Heidelberg, who showed little understanding as to why I had chosen to associate with Itzig Faitel Stern. Those rumors were mainly connected to Faitel's money, for Faitel Stern was enormously rich. At that time Heidelberg was a very small city, and the students played such a conspicuous role there that the appearance of Itzig Faitel Stern and everything in his orbit became the talk of the town. And, to put it more succinctly, Faitel Stern was a kind of Casper Hauser: here was a man, then, who emanated directly from the stingy, indiscriminate, stifling, dirty-diapered, griping and grimacing bagatelle of his family upbringing, and as a result of a hasty decision, with his pockets full of money, was suddenly thrown onto the great pavement of life in a European city, and there he began to look around, ignorant, with blundering movements. Consequently, he was beheld with ridicule and astonishment.

But the matter could not continue like this. Soon after the beginning of our acquaintance, I made some suggestions to Faitel in regard to changing him and making him more modern, and I found that he was receptive to these remarks. Hopefully I have not forgotten to mention that we both studied medicine. The fact that Faitel chose this discipline as his field of study was, after all that we know about his appearance, certainly a propitious *testimonium intellectus*.

"Faitel," I said to him one day, "you must change your way of walking. You are completely convoluted. And this is why you're mocked and ridiculed by everyone in the city!"

"So wot can I do? You tink dis don't make me depressed?" Faitel exclaimed and stamped his flat feet helplessly but with a great show of force on the floor. "I was walking dis way my life long. Mine fadder goes like dis too und hiss de alte Stern Solomon. Geeve me sum new legs. I should pay vat it costs!"

"Yes, pay!" I cried out. "That would be the right thing to do. But who could possibly straighten out your rickety bones?"

We agreed that we had to seek the advice of an orthopedist.

However, the worthy representative of this discipline declared that Itzig was too old and that his bone structure had become too set. Yet, he recommended Professor Klotz, Heidelberg's famous anatomist, who might conduct a scientific examination of Itzig's skeletal framework. So we visited this famous man, and he made all sorts of measurements on Itzig's naked body, had him walk back and forth and finally clapped his hands over his head. Never in his life had he seen such a thing! Then he took out a well-known book, Meyer's *Statistics and Mechanics of Human Anatomy*, Leipzig, 1873. He had been commissioned to write the second edition, and he was displeased because he felt that he now had to revise the entire book after examining Itzig. At this point he asked whether it was certain that Itzig's parentage was human. Of course, this could be proven without a doubt. "Then," Professor Klotz closed his remarks, "I may be forced to abandon all hope. It may be possible to restore the joints of the student Stern so that they all simulate human forms of motion. However," the famous anatomist hesitated, "the means and ways . . ."

"I'll pay wot you shood want," Faitel interjected quickly, possessed by a sudden presentiment. "I'll pay hit. I'll gung pay for mine new statue. So de Herr Professor, he'll hev de geld, alot of geld-era. Deradáng! Deradáng! (to be spoken with a long stress) I'll gonna payera! Deradáng! Deradáng!" Spreading of the hands at shoulder length; bobbing of the head into the vest; rocking of the upper body like a pendulum; smiling positions of the mouth; upper row of teeth exposed; rich amount of saliva.

Now hard times arrived for Faitel. Night and day he hung in traction so that his scoliotic bones could be stretched by his own body weight. Or he was stuck in a cast built like a corset. The nape of his neck was shortened and tightened through a bloody operation to allow Faitel a view of the heavens. The bones which had been reassembled in a new harness had to be exercised and reformed week after week with the help of a gymnast. Faitel had to have private lessons since nobody wished to exercise with him. It was impossible for anyone to make use of these exercises for private purposes, nor did anyone want to see Faitel perform his neck-breaking exercises. Enormous sums of money wandered into the hands of the gymnasts, trainers, orthopedists, and those of Professor Klotz, who directed and supervised everything. After three months the results were mediocre. Naturally the bow-legs remained the same during all these corrective attempts since there had been no possibility to place counterweights in a deeper position and stretch them out. Faitel's advisors were able to calm him down by explaining to him that such legs were also to be found among other classes of human beings such as bakers, etc. But Faitel was indefatigable. Ever since his pointed chin stopped drilling into the breast-plated tie, he had made the firm decision "to become such a fine gentilman just like a goymenera and to geeve up all fizonomie of Jewishness."

About that time a daring operation became known which was called *brisement forcé*. A crooked bone was intentionally broken and treated as an accidental breaking of the leg with the exception that the two pieces were healed in a straight direction. This method was employed in an operation on Faitel Stern's bow-legs. The consequences and incidental circumstances of this cure led to Faitel's being bed-ridden for many weeks at a time for each leg, with all kinds of pain and bandages and enormous costs for a process which at that time necessitated a doctor to come from Paris and perform everything according to the proper specifications.

Old Solomon Stern sent check after check, which was gladly honored by every businessman. Then there were weeks and weeks of attempts to walk with the freshly healed limbs of his body. And really, when Faitel Stern now went out for the first time, one could see that he had made great progress. He had become somewhat taller and resembled a respectable human being. Everything was and still remained stiff for a long time, but he could now pretend to be a normal human being. His face stood straight as a candle. His chin revealed itself now to be terribly long and pointed. His chicken breast was flattened out, and the lapels of his coat ran straight down. In order to prevent Faitel's customary bobbing of his upper body, which was always accompanied by his nasal gurgling "Deradáng! Deradáng!," a barbed wire belt similar to a collar was placed around his hips on his bare skin (as they do with dogs) so that he was immediately spiked when he tended to move up and down or from side to side. Faitel Stern bore all this heroically and stood straight and tall like a pine tree. Yet, only now did the major problem arise. It was clear that one could not introduce him in high society with his speech, of which we have already been given some samples, for it was the mode of expression of an oily, base, cowardly character. And though it was merely a question of changing his outward appearance, it was important to complete this change as soon as possible. Since it was hopeless to raise the level of his Palatinate-Yiddish to that of the related pure high German, an attempt was made to bring his former sing-song on the right track through its direct opposite. A private tutor was engaged, and Itzig was to repeat his clear nasal-sounding manner of speech like a schoolboy, sentence by sentence, so that he learned high German like a totally new, foreign language. Moreover, some students from Hannover were employed to provide company for Itzig in exchange for payment of tuition and diverse meals during one whole semester. This series of measures was the result of expert opinion gathered from the most famous linguist of that time in nearby Tübingen. In addition, a Heidelberg physiologist was brought in for consultation. These gentlemen proceeded from the following considerations: In our brain there is just one part for the speech faculties, and it is used either on the left or right side. It is not impossible to make use of those faculties which have not been used to form a new speech aptitude, and this often takes place quite naturally, for example, after an illness. In such attempts, it is of utmost importance that one makes certain there is nothing in the formation of words and sounds of the new speech which recalls the old idiom otherwise confusion will arise. As the Tübingen specialist expressed it, a new speech island had to be formed in Itzig. And now he was examined to determine which German dialect contained the least tonal affinity with Faitel's Palatinate-Yiddish. At first, the specialists considered Pomeranian. But this was too difficult for Faitel. Finally, they agreed upon the Hannoverian dialect. My reader can well imagine that all these fine diagnostics cost a barrel of money, for these speech exercises were to continue for another entire semester.

It is impossible for me to give the reader an account of all the garnishings, changes, injections and quackeries to which Itzig Faitel Stern submitted himself. He experienced the most excruciating pain and showed great heroism so he could become the equivalent of an Occidental human being. He continually watched for new things, studied secret Christian traits, copied distortions of the mouth, puffed cheeks and gestures, and imagined himself to be part of the heroic Teutonic genre like some young stalwart, blond and naïve, who walked about smiling with great ignorance. Naturally, the tint—the wheat color of Faitel's skin—had to yield to a fine, pastel lead tint, which Itzig learned to exhibit in a superb way. I suspect—it's just a suspicion—that Faitel once nourished himself four weeks in a row on a drug about which I know nothing. It takes the form of a vegetable, and Faitel may have done this to attain the Caucasian color of skin in a natural way. One relatively simple and harmless procedure which, nevertheless, had a gruesome effect concerned his hair. Right about that time, the English bleaches came into fashion. To be sure, since they were secret formulas, they were extremely expensive, but they did change each and every strand of dark hair into magnificent golden blond. The first English beauticians were traveling around Germany at that time, and one of them had settled down in rich Heidelberg, which was always frequented by people from high society. Faitel was one of the first ones to undergo the treatment. So Itzig's coal black curly locks, under which there had always been a suspiciously smelling sweat, were changed into the golden locks of a child. These locks were then straightened out into long Germanic strands by means of a painful process. In addition, Faitel was given a simple North German hairdo, and—finally, the dumb, awkward German lad was complete, a replica of the figure portrayed at times by Schwind in his paintings. He called himself Siegfried Freudenstern and had his matriculation forms and other papers changed.

Faitel was now an entirely new human being. The last treatments—he was very careful—had been completed during the university vacation period near the city and had changed him to such an extent that he was unrecognizable. It was suggested that he attend another university now, but he rejected this idea, mainly because he wanted to remain near Professor Klotz, who was still in charge of the entire psycho-physical operation. And, in fact, since the bleaching of his hair to gold, Faitel was no longer recognized in Heidelberg. He made his appearance there as the son of a Hannoverian landowner and moved in the finest circles of high society. He exercised the North German rasping sound with playful ease, and this scored an extraordinary success wherever he went.

However, Faitel's ambition mounted even higher. —"Faiteles! Such a bootiful yid, such a fine yid! Such a elegant yid!" —This was the way Faitel frequently spoke to himself when he stood in front of a mirror, but only in his thoughts. —"So you tink now you're a Chreesten, wit no drop Jewishness? You tink you could go wearevver you want wot you shood take a seat wit de fine peeple wot everyone should tink: dat's one of us!" —Faitel knew that it had not yet come to this. Yes, whatever pomade, make-up, white buckram, some yards of worsted, cotton, and some varnish could accomplish with a human being, all this had been accomplished with Faitel. But what did everything look like inside?

Did Faitel have a soul? This question was debated everywhere for months by all those people, educators, and doctors who had something to do with him. Of course, the soul necessary for expression of a few hypocritical sentences such as a marriage vow or for throwing a few silver coins to a poor devil at the right moment—Faitel possessed this soul just like everyone else. But Faitel had heard about the chaste, undefined Germanic soul, which shrouded the possessor like an aroma. This soul was the source of the possessor's rich treasures and formed the *shibboleth* of the Germanic nations, a soul which was immediately recognized by all who possessed one. Faitel wanted to have this soul. And, if he could not have genuine eau de cologne, then he wanted the imitation. At the very least, he wanted to appropriate this soul in all its expressions and daily manifestations. So he was advised to go to England, where the purest effusion of this Germanic soul was to be found. Language difficulties soon caused these plans to be dropped. A well-known educator felt that one could reach this higher goal on the basis of a general spiritual predisposition even with Faitel's present one. The famous Cambridge Professor Stokes had only recently published his *Psychological Researches,* in which he explained the primary spiritual predisposition of people like Faitel not as a *spiritual* possession but as a mechanical function or "rotation work," as he called it. This new theory led to the abandonment of all further attempts to cultivate Itzig Faitel's soul.

Once during these tests and examinations Itzig burst out with a question about the dwelling place of the soul. They had to explain to him that ever since Descartes had made the unsuccessful attempt to locate the abode of the soul in the pineal gland of the brain, nobody had tried to locate this spiritual power. Rather, attempts had been made to understand the soul from the combined effects of certain physical and spiritual functions. Since these functions were dependent in a particular manner on the quality of blood, it was possible to assert to a certain degree that the abode of the soul could be located in the blood and its changing condition. Right then Faitel conceived a plan for one of his most daring treatments. Some days after this discussion he was overheard talking joyously to his most intimate associates: "I gonna buy me sum Chreesten blud! I gonna buy me sum Chreesten blud!" This was how he spoke, despite the fact that his advisors had strictly forbidden him to speak this way.

My readers will shake their heads. But you must not forget that Itzig Faitel Stern was a medical student and knew all about the most recent developments in the field. And, furthermore, this is the place to remind you that at that time, when our story was taking place, blood transfusions became fashionable. The rich blood from a body filled to the lymphs was injected into a supine organism poor in blood by opening an exterior blood vessel in the arm. These operations were extremely dangerous and have already been abandoned today. Faitel was strongly advised not to proceed with this, but he would not be deterred. Meanwhile, there were great difficulties to be overcome. Approximately six to eight hardy people had been found who were each to give a liter of blood in exchange for a great deal of money. Yet, when they heard that their blood was destined for a Jew, they withdrew their offer and spoke about the blood spilt on the Cross because of the Jews. They could not be convinced to change their minds. Only when seven strong women from the Black Forest, who had come to the country fair, were persuaded that it was time again to be bled could the major difficulty be settled. Faitel himself made the incision in an adjoining room, and since the amount of blood to be emptied had been exactly prescribed, he had the opened artery punctured in a warm bath until he became unconscious. He wanted to shed his "Jewishness" and let everything run out that could run out. Eight liters of blood from the strong peasant women were then gradually and carefully injected into him during the course of the afternoon. After many days in a coma, Faitel survived this dangerous treatment unscathed. However, he never allowed himself to be thoroughly questioned about its success and the psychological effect. It appeared that it had not been very great, for after a few weeks we found him again making new attempts to gain possession of the German soul.

Thus, he began reciting pathetic and sentimental passages by poets, especially in the social gatherings of the ladies' salons, and he astutely observed the position of the mouth, breath, twinkle of the eyes, gestures, and certain sighs that emanated so passionately and strenuously from German breasts satiated with feelings. To be sure, when the ladies from the aesthetic gatherings did not boost his ego enough, Faitel had actors come to Heidelberg from the nearby court in Darmstadt, heroes and lovers, and he learned Romeo soliloquies with them. To tell the truth, this was more successful than other experiments. Now Faitel could express statements with great adroitness in a discussion such as, "Oh, I must confess, when I reflect about this, when I consider this, everything seems gloomy to me, and my heart shudders." These words would be accompanied by some brusque movements, both hands pressed on the left side of the breast. It was really a very clever way to pour out emotions. Of course, his eyes would rest lifelessly in their sockets like rotten cherries. Yet, he was able to deceive many people. He learned to inhale and exhale superbly. And one time he had the satisfaction of hearing from a student in the ladies' salons that Siegfried Freudenstern was a man with soul through and through.

But Faitel still had a lot of other, old inherited habits, ways of thinking, comical manners, and eccentricities. On our frequent evening walks he liked to meditate and—I'm not sure whether he wanted to recapitulate his religious lessons or mock his former teachers—he would begin to talk with an altered, carping Rabbi's voice examining himself in the following manner: "What doth Jehovah do at the beginning of the day?" —Then Faitel would answer himself in his own voice, but with a fresh witty accent: "He studieth the commandments!" Again the first voice: "What doth the holy Lord do thereafter?" Second voice: "Thereafter he sitteth and ruleth the entire world!" "What doth Jehovah do after this?" "Thereafter he sitteth and nourishes the entire world!" "What doth he do then?" "Then he sitteth and copulates the men and women!" "How long doth the holy Lord copulate the men and women?" "He copulateth the men and women for three hours!" "What doth the holy Jehovah do then in the afternoon?" "He doth nothing in the afternoon, Jehovah. He rests." "What didst thou say? What doth thou mean? The holy Jehovah doth nothing? What doth he do? What doth Jehovah do in the afternoon? —Huh?" Now it seemed that a remote squeaking voice of a young boy answered him from the last desk in the back of a school room: "The holy Jehovah playeth with Leviathan in the afternoon!" "Naturally," interjected the Rabbi's voice, "he playeth with Leviathan!"

During these walks Faitel would be delighted and act like a wild little boy. When he went beyond the boundaries of the city, Faitel sometimes took out a white handkerchief, hung it around his neck, held the two tips in front and began to let loose with a barrage of song, rolling up and down the scales with a screeching gurgle that had a peculiar jubilant and cheerful character. I had never heard the words before, and he sung until his eyes popped and foam was on his lips. Then he almost threw up and meandered next to me along the way like a drunkard. When he came to his senses again, he remained silent and introspective, acted secretively and appeared to be inundated by some unknown happiness.

Naturally his advisors were not to know anything about this since they had forbidden all exercises, sounds, and gestures that might remind him of his former predisposition. Yet I also suspected that Faitel, when he was alone, was still up to some mischief. During the day he was in the European corset, harnessed, supervised, under great surveillance. But in the evening, when he was no longer bound, when he took off the barbed belt and lay in bed, I'm sure he rocked as he formerly did, the pelvis moving back and forth, his hands spreading into the vest pockets, his tongue gurgling and bawling, "Deradáng! Deradáng!" And the entire Palatinate-Yiddish deluge could not be checked.

But Faitel still had other things that were even more ineradicable because, unlike movements, they were not controlled by one's will. Rather, they were lodged in his imagination. Now, in order to present a full picture, I am compelled to touch upon something distasteful: Faitel had a fear of the toilet. He believed in the old Hebrew spirits of the latrine and squalor who bothered people during their most urgent calls. These spirits could take possession of a person and could only be repulsed by certain prayers. However, since Faitel no longer knew these prayers nor could say any of them with conviction, his fear grew even greater. And only the fact that the spirits did not dare attack anyone in the presence of a third party enabled Faitel to dispose of such urgent business in peace—naturally, only after he always provided for the proper conditions.

Such was Faitel's new formation and transformation. Internally there was much that had not been filled by new things, old functions which were still in operation. Externally everything had been smoothed out, combed spic-and-span, thoroughly conditioned, and ready to go. All in all, Faitel and his tutors, advisors, and instructors should have been satisfied with what they had accomplished. Yet Professor Klotz, whose concerned eye watched over his human work with growing interest from semester to semester, may have had mixed feelings when he congratulated himself. Either he felt like a circus director, who had finally tamed a difficult horse for the ring, or he felt like the sublime Creator, who had managed to blow life into a cold lump of clay. After all, hadn't Klotz also blown new life into a distorted bag of broken bones?

Only one thing was still missing, for it was also important to reproduce this human race, which it had cost so much to achieve. The new breed was to be grafted with the finest Occidental sprig. A blonde Germanic lass had to help preserve the results that had been garnered through fabulous efforts. This was the way it sounded in theory. In practice, this meant that the poor, but beautiful flaxen-haired daughter of a civil servant, Othilia Schnack, was to become engaged to the enormously rich son of a landowner, Siegfried Freudenstern. This was what was agreed upon, and it met with Faitel's approval. Indeed, Old Solomon Stern, who sat quietly in his village of Patzendorf in the Palatinate, bought some property near Hannover to serve as the next residence for the young couple. The Hannover students, who had already acted superbly as speech instructors at one time, were to provide the necessary introductions to families in the city and district of Hannover when the time came. Some shaky mortgages on the parental homes of these young men in question were scheduled for foreclosure by Old Solomon sitting in Patzendorf in case they did not cooperate. An exceedingly fabulous trousseau was ordered from the best retailers of Heidelberg in case the wedding ties were indeed to be knotted. In turn, this put extra pressure on the business circles in this university city. One talked so much about the engagement it finally meant that the knots had to be tied. Or, this engagement could not be allowed to be dissolved, as though there had already been one at all. The young lady in question, Othilia, had light starry eyes and was an open, lovely creature, but she had a strong woman's intuition. She did not feel entirely comfortable in the presence of the golden blond youth who purred as he spoke. She sensed something eerie but could not confirm her suspicion. Her father, a fearful man, who had worked himself up from a scribe to a middle-grade official through good behavior and honesty, was very anxious. He always obeyed, never said no, walked with tiny steps as though trotting, carried his chin and neck hidden in an unstarched, open-collared shirt, and as soon as he noticed that something like a family meeting was to take place, he grabbed his hat and cane and went for a walk. Her mother, a big-breasted, ponderous housekeeper who could be charming every now and then, but most of the times was energetic and industrious, was for the marriage. She already possessed earrings with gems as large as pigeon eggs as a gift from Faitel Stern. This clever woman was only suspicious of the entire affair because the Heidelberg professors, especially the professors of medicine, took such a lively interest in bringing about the marriage. Naturally, the hotel owners, wine merchants, clothiers, embroiderers, bakers, jewelers, printers, negotiators, coachmen, and porters were for the marriage. The Protestant clergy—Othilia was Protestant—also gave a nod of approval to the entire project. The fact that nobody had met any of Faitel's relatives caused some consternation in the Schnack family. However, word had it that the parents were well advanced in years. And the long journey from Hannover! If only a brother, or better yet, a sister of the groom could have appeared on the scene! But the cawing nest back in Patzendorf naturally took care not to utter a peep.

Faitel was now in his sixth semester. His knowledge and good performances were praised. Still, it caused some sensation when it became known that Professor Klotz had appointed the young student from Hannover as his assistant right after he had been granted his degree. This appointment required the confirmation of the ministry in Karlsruhe. It came. Consequently, fuel was now added in Karlsruhe to the flaming rumor about the rich marriage that was going to take place in Heidelberg. The reigning sovereign could not but help hear all this talk. And one day the director of Schnack's office informed the man with a melting smile that one had talked about his daughter's forthcoming marriage—in Karlsruhe—at the court. Now the peak had been reached! The old scribe kept quiet and held his head stiff behind his tie. His two dry lips tipped with a black-stubbed Kaiser moustache could not even gasp for breath until the tall, haggard director with long coat-tails disappeared from sight. Then old Schnack threw the feather pen on his desk, spraying some ink in the process, grabbed his hat and cane, and rushed home coughing along the way. "At the court! At the court!" Now there was no stopping it. Poor Othilia, who shuddered upon hearing this, sobbed, threw herself into the arms of her mother, and declared that she would obey. Her mother immediately sent a message to the newly appointed assistant Dr. Freudenstern, and the wedding day was scheduled.

Now, my dear reader, I should like to have a word with you. Did you ever hear of people wearing a coat in the winter with its collar and lapels topped with fur to make others believe that the entire coat is lined this way? A trivial thing! A small weakness! Do you also wear a coat like this? Oh, then throw it away if you're a man. Otherwise, the fur will trip your tongue one day when you're most in need of a breath of air. (However, if you're a woman, you may wear it.) But that little bit of fur, there's so much talk about it, isn't that true? —Good! —Still, haven't you seen people, my dear reader, who wear such furs around their souls in order to conceal their porous and shabby constitution? And then they act as though they had a noble soul clad in the finest of fabrics. Oh, what a shame! Oh, the squalor and pity of it all! What if some well-behaved, open soul still clad in its confirmation suit, now somewhat snug, were to have trouble or to be deceived! —Perhaps you yourself, my reader, possess such wrappings for your soul? Oh, then throw this book in a corner if you're a man and spew everything out! This is not for you. Only a woman may lie and cloak herself in false wrappings.

Perhaps, my dear reader, you have seen animals talking among themselves. Two pigeons or two roosters, two dogs or even two foxes? Do you think they understand each other? Certainly! Certainly! Each knows what the other wants in a flash. But two people? When they stretch their heads toward one another, sniff and peep at each other and then begin their facial magic tricks, blinking, ogling, rubbing, chewing thin air, and whimpering "fiddlesticks" and "the devil!"—what are they doing? Do they actually understand each other? Impossible! They don't want to. They can't and are not allowed to. The lie prevents them from doing this. Oh, horse manure and stinky resin, you are gems in comparison to what comes out of people's mouths!

When Prometheus finally had permission from God to make human beings, it occurred only on the express humiliating condition that they had to have one quality which made them much lower than animals. Prometheus, who was only in a rush to see his artwork finished, agreed to this. It was the lie. Oh, base contract that allowed us all to be born under the same sign of the lie! And were you perhaps the cause for that lying tower of Babel forcing people to separate because they no longer understand each other in spite of the coughing and gesticulating? And, even if the German nations were the last to be created, received the least repercussions from all this because so much of the lying substance had already been used up by the previous Asiatic and Latin races, there is still enough there. —Oh, reader, if you can, spit out this dirt like rotten slime, and show your lips, your tongue, and your teeth just as they are! —And now listen to the conclusion of Faitel's comedy.

In the Inn of the White Lamb, which was on the Martergasse in Heidelberg, the large hall was filled with a radiant group of people who had witnessed the wedding ceremony of Othilia Schnack with Siegfried Freudenstern. It had been a long time since something like this had been seen in this university city. I'm not certain whether the civil ceremony had been preceded by a church wedding. Most likely. The papers testifying that Freudenstern was Protestant had been acquired from a Hannover pastor with a sympathetic ear. This I know. Nothing had been missing except for the birth certificate. Yet, many communities in the Lüneberger Heide near Hannover had expressed their joy and readiness to add a name to their birth register, especially the name of such a citizen as Herr Dr. Freudenstern, who immediately made a donation of five thousand guilders to one community for the restoration of the church door.

Even the reader must make an extra effort, now that we have come to the end of this affair, to dismiss "Faitel" from his mind. It is only Freudenstern who is presently the hero of the story! A tall young man with strands of blond hair stands before us, or rather is talking at this moment seated at the table with Professor Klotz, while dessert is about to be served. Of course, the formation of the teeth, the padded lips, the nasal pitch in Faitel's face had to remain absolutely fixed to prevent a monster from becoming visible. And whoever had an eye for such things could recognize the sensual, fleshy, and jutting Sphinx-like face in Freudenstern's profile. However, first of all, not everyone has an eye for such things. Secondly, one does not always look at someone's profile. Thirdly, during a wedding celebration one hardly sees unpleasant things. Fourthly, it was still debatable whether the Egyptian Sphinx-face was of Semitic nature. Fifthly, Klotz had dropped a remark most elegantly during one of his private seminars on anthropology, in which he was giving students information about the determination of skull measurements, that Freudenstern's cranium formation was one of the purest specimens among all the examples known to him, and that it corresponded closest to the head formation of the Hermunduren, who had been the earliest historically known inhabitants of Germany.

Just then, the pudding was brought out. The friendly innkeeper of the White Lamb went around the table of feasting guests in a sweat and counted and counted, for he was to be paid one ducat per person excluding the wine. The menu did not entirely meet his taste and did not suit, so he believed, the reputation of a first-class inn like the White Lamb. As owner of the establishment, he had demanded a pure French menu. The predominantly German character of the wedding banquet was the result of Klotz's express orders. Yes, even sauerkraut was served, and in his desperation the innkeeper tried to offset this German vulgarity by giving it the French appellation *choucroute*. There were selected morsels of pork, and fatty sparkling rinds gleamed from all the trays entrenched as *entremets* in the middle of the table for the entire evening. Freudenstern sat between the bride, who was pale as wax, and Klotz. Across from them were the Schnacks. The flabby skin of old man Schnack's face seemed to pull back, frightened by the wasteful quantities of food piled up in front of him, and he looked with astonishment through his large silver-framed monocle at these people who were well-versed in consummation. A stand-up collar with a shining white tie held in the correct position his long neck with the dug-out larynx. A medal sparkled on his tidy, black double-breasted jacket. It had arrived the evening before from Karlsruhe. Moreover, Schnack

was addressed repeatedly as "Herr Councillor of the Chancel-
lery." Frau Schnack, with her embonpoint covered by elegant
gray silk, shook her head energetically back and forth. The gems
as large as pigeon eggs waddled on her ears. There was a cloud
of fetid medicine over this part of the table.—Dessert was still
being served.

Now, dear reader, prepare yourself! Something extraordinary
appears to be in the making. A sultry atmosphere was forming
in the room, like one you feel when a storm is about to break.
A great deal of wine had been drunk. Moreover, Faitel, who had
been congratulated by everyone, had to make toasts time and
again. I don't know whether Faitel could hold a great deal of
alcohol. The customs of his race indicate moderation. On the
other hand, it is known that if you inundate the brain with
spirits, they may not only generate critical explosions in the
psychological and motor sensories of humans but also open up
parts of the brain, or rather, zones of memory, which, without
the influx of the combustible substance, would normally remain
quiet for a long time, perhaps for eternity. As I said, I don't
know whether Faitel was accustomed to drinking. What I do
know is that Faitel had discarded the barbed belt, the preserva-
tive of his correct posture, for the first time right before this
celebration. Nobody can reprimand him for this, since the discarding was symbolic. Faitel had entered Christian society for
good on this day. Furthermore, the smart female reader will
comprehend that a wedding day is followed by a wedding night
which consists of a wedding disrobement so that this strange
ornamental object had to be removed from the eyes of the tearful
bride.

But now the time has finally come to inform the reader that
Faitel had been sitting rigid and motionless for about ten minutes
and gaping directly under the table. His face turned crimson at
times and then white as chalk. He seemed to be occupied with

entirely different thoughts that expanded and entranced him without his help. But not without the help of many glasses of cliquot that he hurriedly gulped down and that the concerned innkeeper quickly filled one after the other since the wine was not included in the cover price.

Faitel raised his right hand from time to time and made a gesture with his index finger as though he wanted to say "Psst! Psst!" so he could hear his inner voice better, for there was still a great tumult, clanging of plates, and chatter in the room. Nobody had an inkling about the wondrous experiment that the avenging angel was in the process of preparing. Faitel appeared to add to this in a very systematic and purposeful way by pouring down champagne as one shoots oil onto a flame which is at the point of extinction. When it seemed that the illumination that glowed within him was about to fizzle, he slowly brought his upper body against the table, stretched out his right hand without regarding it, grabbed the filled glass, drank it down, and then raised his finger as though he wanted to say: "Listen, is it coming"—And it came. The contents of this frenetic chain of thoughts seemed to be more cheerful and dynamic, for Faitel slapped himself with the flat of his hands on his thighs a few times making a loud smack, and he laughed and giggled to himself. Those people who had a good ear could already hear now a few "Deradángs! Deradángs!" But the guests were not at all aware, as the reader is, about the meaning of "Deradáng!" And the joking, laughing, and toasting of drinks drowned out the first warning sounds to a great extent. Klotz was involved in a lively discussion with his neighbor on the left. Only the bride on the right observed these early symptoms of delirium with composure and curiosity. Faitel's chin drilled itself deeper and deeper into his breast in its rigid position so that it finally assumed that crippled-looking compulsive formation familiar to the reader from the early part of the story. The people closest to

Faitel, among them Frau Schnack, who was quick to understand what was happening, were now forced to take notice of him. However, they seemed to want to attribute everything to a peculiar mood that had come over him.—"Waiererá! . . ." Faitel screamed suddenly with a rasping, vibrating voice. "Waiererá!—Champagnererá!—So *nu*, wot's de metter?—So vy shoodn't I hev notink to drink?—I vant you shood know dat I'm a human bing jost as good for sumtink as any ov you!"

Now everyone's attention in the room was immediately drawn to him. Even the waiters carrying the large piles of dishes came to a stop and stared at the middle of the rows of tables where a bloodthirsty, swelling, crimson visage spewed saliva from flabby drooping lips, and gushing eyes glared at them. Everyone seemed to be under a magic spell, and nobody knew what to do. Even Klotz lost his composure and looked with horror at the Jew next to him.

Faitel's glass had been filled once again by the innkeeper, who stood behind him. While terrified and sympathetic forces focused on him from all directions, Faitel himself began to speak with a squeaky and entirely different tone of voice. "What doth he do in the next three hours, the holy Jehovah?—Deradáng! Deradáng!" With one quick swoop, his thumbs were in the pockets of his wedding vest. Now he bobbed back and forth and gave an infatuated look at the heavens.—Again with a changed voice giving the answer: "He sitteth and copulateth the men and women!" Again the first voice: "How long doth the holy Lord copulate the men and women?" the same *positur*; lascivious movements back and forth on the chair; jumping up and down, gurgling, clicking of the tongue.—The voice answering: "Three hours long doth he copulate the men and women!" First voice: "What doth he do in the afternoon, the holy Jehovah? Deradáng! Deradáng!"—Answer: "He doth nothing, Jehovah. He taketh a rest!" First voice: "What didst thou day? What doth thou mean?

The holy Jehovah doth nothing? What doth he do? What doth Jehovah do in the afternoon? Huh?"—A young boy's voice from the distance: "The holy Jehovah playeth with Leviathan in the afternoon!"—The first voice interjects triumphantly: "Naturally! He playeth with Leviathan!"

At this moment Faitel jumped from his chair, began clicking his tongue, gurgling, and tottering back and forth while making disgusting, lascivious and bestial canine movements with his rear end. "Deradáng! Deradáng!" He jumped around the room. "I done bought for me Chreesten blud! Waitererá, vere iss mine copulated Chreesten bride? Mine briderá! Geeve me mine briderá! I vant you shood know dat I'm jost a Chreesten human bing like you all. Not von drop of Jewish blud!—Wot misery! Vere is mine briderá?"

Everyone scattered. The terrifying visage drove the young ladies from the room. Those people who remained behind watched with horror as Faitel's blond strands of hair began to curl during the last few scenes. Then the curly locks turned from red to dirty brown to blue-black. The entire glowing and sweaty head with tight gaunt features was once again covered with curly locks. In the meantime it appeared that Faitel had peculiar difficulties and struggled with his exalted movements. His arms and legs, which had been stretched and bent in numerous operations, could no longer perform the recently learned movements, nor the old ones. Moreover, the paralyzing effect of the alcohol made itself quickly felt. To be sure, Klotz had cried for ice packs, but it was in vain. Everyone saw that this was a catastrophe which could no longer be prevented. The beautiful Othilia sought refuge in the arms of her mother. Everyone looked with dread at the crazy circular movements of the Jew. The ignominious end, which is the fate of all drunkards, befell Faitel, too. A terrible smell spread in the room, forcing those people who were still hesitating at the exit, to flee while holding their noses. Only

Klotz remained behind. And finally, when even the feet of the drunkard were too tired to continue their movements, Klotz's work of art lay before him crumpled and quivering, a convoluted Asiatic image in wedding dress, a counterfeit of human flesh, Itzig Faitel Stern.

The Operated Goy
(1922)

he Count von Rehsok's family was accustomed to boasting a great deal about the indisputable purity of a racial bloodline that had been documented for centuries. It could be proven that a Rehsok had already distinguished himself in a stunning way during Titus's destruction of Jerusalem. Ever since then, the struggle against the Jewish plague, which had threatened to wipe out the frail Aryans, had been joined by each and every respectable count in the Rehsok line as though it were his privilege. In fact, the Rehsoks supplied parliament with the most eloquent leaders of the anti-Semitic movement, and they especially inveighed against the Jewish-Ayrian mix-breeds, who had succeeded in marrying into the Prussian aristocracy and even in poisoning the milieu of the king with the pestilential stench of their misbegotten blood.

Every Aryan child knows what a Jew looks like. Indeed, every domestic pet can scent out a Jew. If one carefully abstracted certain elements from each Jewish and each Oriental type, then one would be left with the type representative of the counts of Rehsok: they did not wear corkscrew locks; rather, their hair was soft and wavy, almost silvery blond. Their white foreheads dropped steeply like walls of granite instead of sinking and slanting toward the rear. They were suspicious of so-called eagle noses, for their noses were unbelievably straight. They all had thin lips, Prussian chins, proud necks, and fabulously slender builds, and their legs, which in their innocence did not know either X or O, stood simultaneously on aristocratic and pan-Germanic feet and took strides as though descending from Mount Olympus. Above all, they did not have narrow eyes with a dark brown glow but open, true blue ones which glistened like pure ice, and the power of their imperious look was enhanced exceedingly by the monocle.

Now, at the proper time Count Kreuzwendedich Rehsok travelled to Bonn in order to be with his noble relatives, the Borussians, and to spend a couple of semesters studying at the university before following the traditional path of a military career. Upon his departure his parents, siblings, aunts, and uncles kept warning him, for God's sake, not to throw his life away on a worthless woman: "Keep your blood pure! There are now enormously rich Semitic daughters who are keen on our kind. Sometimes they're not exactly bad looking—on the contrary. But it would be a disgrace to our noble heritage if one of us were to keep just one of them as a mistress."

As if such warnings were at all necessary for Kreuzwendedich! He was so much above and beyond this that he had promised his father he would order all his articles and utensils only from strict anti-Semitic manufacturers if at all possible. Whatever was around him, whatever he touched had to be completely cleansed of Jewishness and remain that way. For instance, he had a Bible produced in which all the Hebrew names were translated into German. Consequently, the wise Solomon was called the wise

Friedrich. Incidentally, his favorite literature was not the Bible but Nordic mythology. His noble head was filled with Odin and his entourage. His future wife was to be called Frigga; his children *in spe*, Balder, Braga, Hermod, Thor and Tyr. He had given the name Audumbla to a cow in his father's barn and called his little castle Muspelheim. His servant responded to the giant's name Bor and was, in truth, a giant in stature. Moreover, Kreuzwendedich kept two trained ravens and called them Hugin and Munin. As was the case with all such lordly men, Count Rehsok also had a latent aversion toward Christianity, "that Jewish offshoot of an Indian tribe."

This, then, was the Count Kreuzwendedich Rehsok, who went to Bonn, where he mixed only with a few Borussians from the high aristocracy, remained silent most of the time, and if he talked, only in the style of a telegram. The giant Bor needed just half a word to guess what he meant. "Take walk! Clean street! Signal before! Swastika! Detour!" In good grammatical German this meant: Bor was to accompany him on a walk, and if anyone or anything Jewish showed up, he was to give him a signal so that he could make a detour around the Jewish schools or synagogues. And Bor was to stick a swastika on the arm of his coat. This was the way the cavalier strutted through the streets with the customary white student cap on his blond parted hair, his monocle on his eye, followed by his livery servant in a set distance. As soon as anything Hebrew showed itself, the servant made a shrill sound with a silver whistle. Of course, it would be superfluous to remark that the Count's Great Dane was carefully trained to bite any Jew who came too close. In addition, the raven Hugin could correctly chirp the well-known Borkum anti-Semitic hymn.

In the meantime, word got around about the young count's behavior, which was an immense delight to the Germanic families of the city. Even the quarrelsome Jewish children learned about it so that it was unavoidable that certain extraordinarily delicate ears would also hear about it. Indeed, Rebecca Gold-Isaac, a languishing odalisque with eyes like almonds, ebony hair, ivory skin, etcetera, etcetera, became tremendously upset because the count had become the talk of the town. "I'm going to buy me this pompous turkey," she decided for herself, "even if I have to marry him out of revenge."

Her papa was practically a billionaire. Therefore, it was immensely easy to transform Rebecca Gold-Isaac into the Baroness Freia-Rotraut von Isagold and to bestow upon her head a bronze wig like something painted by Titian. And yet, despite it all, she still had difficulty crossing the path that the count took on his walks with Bor whistling, the Great Dane snapping, and the fluttering raven, which Bor handled like a falcon, piping the customary hymn. So imperturbably sure of their purpose were they that their instincts functioned here perfectly despite her disguise. However, one time they were just a split second too late. And this split second was just enough for a veritable Count Rehsok—but patience, we are getting ahead of our story. . . .

Dazzled by the beauty of the young woman born Gold-Isaac, Bor almost forgot to whistle, and consequently the raven and the Great Dane almost forgot their duty so that Kreuzwendedich was able to take in the young Jewish woman for half a moment with eyes that were no less dazzled than Bor's. "Parbleu!" He was startled. "Impossible! Especially since nothing smells. *Foetor judaicus* is otherwise infallible."

"Whoever can't smell should feel," retorted Rotraut and lifted a riding whip. Together, Count Rehsok and Bor seized her by the arm. Her cheeks became feverishly crimson, and with a ravishingly beautiful and scornful Medusa-look, she said, "Shame on you!" And she spit her contempt into the count's face, jumped into her carriage that came rolling up to fetch her, and drove away.

This incident, too, became the talk of the town. The Borussians threw mud at Gold-Isaac in front of his palatial mansion. However, love (preferably called eros by people with a finer education) is capricious and likes to unite opposing forces (cf. the Montagues and Capulets). As far as purity of race was concerned, the house of Gold-Isaac was the Jewish counterpart to the family of Count Rehsok: ditto, ever since the destruction of Jerusalem, and ever since the dispersion of the Jewish people in many different countries, the family had never become contaminated by alien blood. To be sure, this fact was passed on more by word of mouth than documents. Whatever the case may be, Count Rehsok had suffered a psychological trauma after gazing upon the beautiful Rebecca or rather Freia-Rotraut, for he had not been spared, and he could not get rid of this trauma because he did not clearly grasp what it was. And it was the same with Rotraut—a half a moment had been enough. Fascinated by his inimical strangeness, she felt hate, vanity, and fury mixed with love. She yearned ardently to overcome everything, that is, she yearned for complete assimilation and incorporation of the enemy. She strengthened her resolve to marry him and thus intended to triumph over him and his clan. Just one look was like lightning and had revealed to her how much power she had over him. Still under the influence of her spit Kreuzwendedich, enchanted by her, was in a trance. To be sure, he knew nothing about his feelings. His "high consciousness" was highly anti-Semitic enough to abhor Rebecca in an honest and unsuspecting way. Nonetheless, she felt and knew perfectly well that she had to become the Countess Rehsok. Nor would she settle for anything less, and if she failed, she would have no other choice but to plunge into the crater of self-despisement. Who knows, then, whether what people call love is nothing more than the reinforcement of one's very own self-confidence? The weak feminine sex desires this reinforcement passionately, while the strong masculine sex enjoys the power of its self-possession doubly or three times to the full through the generous sensual pleasure of concession.

What a problem! Bringing about the reconciliation between the Montagues with the Capulets was child's play in comparison. Freia-Rotraut knew with utmost certainty that she would not be happy until Count Rehsok's offspring sprouted from her Jewish womb. The young count had strange feelings. He lacked something, but he did not like to recall what it was. He did not want to admit to himself that he was lost to the beautiful Jewess. For better or worse, Rebecca had to take the initiative. So she revealed everything to her parents. Mother Gold-Isaac, named Hagar, waddled about and wrung her hands studded with rings. Back and forth she went through three grand parlors, continually crying out, to be sure, in the purest high German: "*Veh is mir,* dear God! My child is *meshu . . .* !"

Papa Gold-Isaac, whose first name was coincidentally Isaac, dealt in *Realpolitik*, and as he sat in his easy chair, half-lying and twiddling his thumbs, he posed phlegmatic questions: "What a situation! It had to be the Rehsoks! If you had asked me, they're all *nebbechs* and rich to boot. I can't buy them for you. There's nothing I can do here. Good, my child, even though my heart is breaking on account of your poor mother—don't sob, Hagar dear—I won't stand in your way. If he has himself circumcised with everything that goes with it, caftan, *payess, tallith* tassels, Rebecca, you can have as many counts as you want. I can buy practically the whole city of Gotha. And, if I have to, I'll get you Rehsok—only he must let himself be circumcised. If not, we'll give you our good Jewish curse so that your womb will wither!"

Rotraut was horrified. Unfortunately, Isaac-Gold belonged to the sect of Birnbaumianers, who believe that the only real Jew is the East European Jew. The cultivated West European Jew, for example, the catholicizing Martin Buber, was already considered a decadent Jew. Freia was faced with a terribly difficult task. What could she do?

Something occurred to her. She sensed with the sharpest feminine intuition that she had captured Kreuzwendedich's heart. Wasn't it precisely the radical despising of Jews that could serve as the most unlikely means to produce the opposite? Couldn't it generate the quickest turnabout to the other extreme? Anti-Semitism is perhaps even more Jewish than Judaism. After all, whoever hates and despises predisposes himself in all secrecy, slowly but surely, for the most intimate ties of blood, indeed, for an identification with the object of his negation. If she could make the young count aware of all this, then she could be sure of him. Of course, the count would first have to feel how necessary it was to be psychoanalyzed.

Rebecca bribed Rehsok's servant Bor much more with her charm than with money and sought contact with feudal aristocrats, who, in turn, influenced the young Rehsok gently but firmly in her interest until the count himself suddenly appeared in the office of the famous Dr. Freud, where the young man displayed some puzzling psychological inhibitions. In response, the authentic destroyer of subterfuges robbed Count Rehsok's psyche of its protective cover in such a sure-handed anatomical way that the count sank with a terrible cry into the arms of his servant who had rushed over to catch him. Then he collected himself, and with inherited bravery, indeed, with a certain boldness, he looked at his fate in the form of the marvelously beautiful Rebecca Gold-Isaac straight in the eye. At first, all this took place only in his imagination, but soon it was also to be in person.

Now he was prepared to surrender body and soul. Rotraut began to dominate him completely and he acquiesced, gnashing his teeth but also with delight. When he made his first visit to the palatial mansion of Gold-Isaac without ravens, Great Dane, and servant, the Borussians held him in ill-repute and sent their first office-bearers to the count's father, who most solemnly called for a family meeting. However, not only did Kreuzwende-dich not appear, but the news also spread that he had become secretly engaged to Rotraut. As a result, the Rehsok clan announced that he was banned and excommunicated. However, he had already reached such a strong mutual understanding with Rotraut that he did not give the slightest care about the banishment. On the contrary, he breathed a sigh of relief. Yet, now that she had got him this far, Rotraut began to reject him. Consequently, he insisted on knowing the reason for her recent withdrawal since he wanted to marry her in a respectable manner.

"First become a Jew, completely Jewish, a Jew to the point of excess, with caftan, phylactery, and long locks of hair. You don't love me with all your heart unless you become utterly Jewish deep in the marrow of your Aryan bones, a Jew and nothing but a Jew. You in particular owe this to us as atonement."

After delivering this ultimatum, Rotraut refused to see him anymore and thereby drove him to commit a most exalted act that arose from his crazed love for her. He began studying Hebrew and had numerous rabbis initiate him into Jewish teachings, prayers, commandments, and customs. He visited many synagogues and other places of worship. Finally, he let himself be officially converted to Judaism and also underwent the fatal cut of the knife that every male Jewish baby, without being asked, tolerates without giving it a thought. Now he was given permission to appear before Rotraut, but he found her unmoved when he, his monocle covering the tears on his eyelash, entered her blue parlor.

"A monocle? —Please, Moses —he was now called Moishe Mogandovidwendedich —drop the monocle! Your Jewish soul hasn't really taken complete hold of the infernal Rehsok body yet! This goyim posture is an insult to the memory of my forefathers. Is that love? Do you think I could stand with you like that under the *chuppa*? Do you think I want to be wed to such a bridegroom looking the way you still look? Until the former Rehsok really looks like a Jewish man, like in the paintings of Steinhardt, Segal, or Chagall, you can forget all about marrying me!"

After saying this, she showed him a picture of two warped young men, whereupon the man, who had now become the actual Moishe, crushed the monocle with one of the heels of his shoes that still clanked a little like a spur.

"You demand the impossible, Rebecca!"

"March!" Rebecca pointed with her index finger. "Go to Professor Friedlaender! He's expecting you and has already been paid to boot!"

Friedlaender was one of the most famous orthopedists around. However, he was now confronted with the perverse task, in a certain way to do the reverse, that is, to act as a caco-orthopedist. He was to transform an aristocratic, valiant figure of Germanic stock into the Jewish intellectual type. The static principle of Rehsok's feudal body was to be convulsed into the Jewish one. So, first, the doctor used the most radical electrical instruments to eliminate the hair from the count's blond head, covered it with a wig of strict Galiziana coiffure, and dyed the eyebrows black. The doctor devoted special attention to the nose, which he endowed with an artificial hump and made the tip curl over. Thereafter, he performed one of his most famous spinal atrophies. The count's bones were broken at their joints and then carefully brought to heal in the shape of an egg. It was in this condition testifying to his change that Count Moishe had himself photographed and used the photograph to present himself to Rebecca and her *mishpocheh* in effigy for the time being. Then he disappeared, with brand new flat feet, to Romania to learn Yiddish from the wonder rabbis there as well as all the gestures that go along with it. He talked with arms, legs, and tongue, a man after Jehovah's own heart. In a letter written in Hebrew he announced to his fiancée's parents that he would soon be making the bridegroom's official visit.

The family cordiality at his reception could not have been more splendid. The marriage date was moved ahead. In order to obtain the inalienable portion of the disinherited Moishe's inheritance, Papa Gold-Isaac mobilized his attorneys, who reached an agreement with the Rehsok family whereby Count Moishe had to discard his aristocratic name. And, what a horror! On this occasion, while they were having a great deal of trouble finding a Jewish name for the count, some jokester discovered that the family name of Count Rehsok was kosher spelled backwards. Thus, under pious laughter Count Kreuzwendedich Rehsok now became and embodied the real stockbroker Moishe Kosher. Rebecca's triumph was boundless, and she made sure that the entire world, especially the people who counted, learned about it. This grotesque affair reached the highest echelons. Indeed, nobody spoke about anything else at the court and in high society.

At the next family gathering of the Rehsok clan, astonishment and rage got the upper hand. They planned to disturb if not hinder the wedding celebration. Nor were they ashamed to stir up the Borussians, who had taken Bor and the two ravens into their employ after they had been discharged by Kosher. At the wedding table in Gold-Isaac's mansion, the close relatives were seated alongside the president of the Jewish congregation. The house organ played music by Mendelssohn and Bruch. After a dozen or so rabbis had blessed the young couple in the synagogue they all held celebration speeches almost at the same time. Moishe Kosher handed Rebecca (it was just the time of Passover) a round *matzoh* to bite, and Rebecca herself was just about to take a bite when—suddenly the giant Bor stormed into the large room and trampled the waiters. He was disguised or rather undisguised as one-eyed Odin, and on his shoulders were the ravens Hugin and Munin, who smartly croaked the Borkum anti-Semitic hymn. All at once the organ became silent.

"God of my fathers!" Moishe Kosher exclaimed, not so incorrectly, and he stood up on his crooked legs, the tallith strangely wrapped around his thighs. Now all the Borussians stormed inside, and there was hand-to-hand combat. The women and girls fled to the gallery and screamed with all their might. Rebecca, always sober, alerted the police by telephone. Gold-Isaac made his way to Odin and stuffed his pockets full with hundred mark bills. "This is for you, my man, and more, if you drive these thugs out of here."

The two ravens flapped their wings and took off from Bor's shoulders like bats from hell zooming toward the tables.

"May God bless whoever has only one eye!" screamed Gold-Isaac. "He's king among the blind goyim."

Bor, nicely financed, helped the Jewish congregation drive the Borussians out of the room, where they fell into the hands of the police. Once they were charged, they had to pay dearly for their actions.

Now Mr. and Mrs. Moishe Kosher are living today as committed Zionists in a country villa near Jerusalem. To be sure their offspring are not called Balder, Braga, Hermond, Tor, and Tyr. Instead, they have more melodic and honest names: Shlaume, Shmul, Feigelche, Pressel, and Yankef. —The Rehsok clan has vainly sought to the present day to change its name and must consequently put up with the fact that, when something is not completely kosher, people in their circles say that it is not completely 'rehsok.'

Since then, anti-Semitism has noticeably slackened. Certain orthopedists are feared and resisted by people who are still proud of the purity of their race. Nevertheless, Professor Friedlaender has enjoyed an enormous increase of clientele. He has an institute that rents out masks, but it does not rent out mere costumes. Rather it produces skin and hair, bones and muscle as disguises. A former emperor from the West recently had himself transformed into a Negro in order to escape the Bolshevist rabble. Czar Nicholas, who had disappeared, is living today as a harmless rabbi in Moishe Kosher's vicinity, and they are on familiar footing with each other. One no longer bases everything dogmatically on racial differences. Racial blood has stopped being considered a special kind of vital juice. Meanwhile, Professor Friedlaender gathers it in bottles and continues to transfer it undauntedly from one vessel into another.

Oskar Panizza: The Operated German as Operated Jew

Writing on Oskar Panizza's 1893 story *The Operated Jew* is like opening a can of choice meat filled with worms. Though the meat might have been prepared well and still have some nutritional value, the worms have poisoned it. Ordinarily one should throw away the entire can, but in the case of Panizza's *The Operated Jew*, it is more important to investigate how the worms came to infect the meat, for the story is surely one of the most repulsive and insightful narratives ever written about German anti-Semitism. It bears the indelible marks of a disturbed and talented author who depended on sickness to keep a "healthy" distance from what he perceived to be a sick Germany.

Panizza's narrative is filled with stunning ambiguities which reflect extreme hatred and fear of Jews, who are both ridiculed and regarded with awe. To add to the ambiguity, Panizza attacked Jews for wanting to be part of a philistine German society and argued that they would be better off by not giving up their peculiar faith and racial characteristics. In a most ingenious fashion, he conceived a fantastic constellation which allowed him to reproduce all the worst stereotypes and attitudes about Jews while criticizing the deplorable development of instrumental rationality in the form of eugenics, the hypocrisy of church and state in Germany, and socialization as a form of operation. From our present "Holocaust consciousness" it is chilling to see how Panizza, no matter how disturbed he was, placed his finger on the sore spots of German-Jewish assimilation at the end of the nineteenth century and anticipated a virtual destruction of Jewish identity due to German and Jewish compliance with the operative social procedures and customs of that time.

Interestingly, two major German-Jewish critics were drawn to Panizza's writings quite early and recognized that he had an uncanny way of uncovering the sick side of Germany. Kurt Tucholsky wrote in 1920 that "very few people know this man today, and his books are for the most part out-of-print. He himself lives in an insane asylum in Franconia where he was brought in 1904. This is Dr. Oskar Panizza, who was the most audacious and daring, the most spirited and revolutionary prophet of his country when he was still in command of his senses. In comparison to him, Heine is nothing but a dried-out lemon. In his struggle against church and state and particularly against the German church and state, he went the limit. He hated Goths and Romans equally, and he hated them with such passion, power, and ardent feelings that the flames of that time still reach and scorch us as though they had been ignited today."[1] In addition to this, Walter Benjamin praised Panizza and compared him to a heretical icon painter who possessed a bilious fanatical manner of satirizing German philistinism.[2]

Both Tucholsky and Benjamin have been joined by other writers[3] over the years who have defended Panizza despite his apparent repugnant features. Yet, it seems to me that it might be more beneficial and even fairer to Panizza to regard him as the sick and tormented man he was. His views on German society were bizarre and reflected primarily his desperate predicament as a paranoid who invited persecution. This also made him acutely aware of pathological socio-cultural tendencies. By studying the manifestations of degenerative impulses in himself and through his art he sought therapeutic release from uncontrollable fears and aggression. In particular, his ambivalent feelings toward Germany were projected in perverse ways so that the sickness cultivated in his art, which was supposedly cathartic for him, usually had a bewildering if not shattering effect on his readers. Almost all his stories and dramas testify to his obsession with social and private pathologies. Panizza ripped the lid off taboo topics and made them the subject of painful scrutiny. On a cultural level, his phobia concerning church and state endowed his stories with an eerie, prophetic quality. Whether they do, indeed, illustrate the sick side of Germany will remain a debatable point. Certainly his story about the operated Jew, which depicted the social problem of anti-Semitism in such a distorted and offensive manner, anticipated significant cultural and political tendencies. In this respect the story has both a documentary and an actual value for contemporary audiences: by fantasizing in a distorted way about his personal dilemma as a German, Panizza touches acutely on the subtle, psychological ways Germans, including German-Jews, have operated on themselves and continue to operate on themselves in various ways.

Born on November 12, 1853 in Bad Kissingen, Franconia, Panizza experienced childhood traumas which were bound to determine his paranoiac and vicious attitudes toward church and state.[4] Upon the death of his Catholic father in 1855, his mother Mathilde, a strong, outspoken woman who wrote religious stories and tracts as a Protestant, defied the local authorities and decided to have Panizza and his brothers and sisters raised as Lutherans. For the next eight years of his life, Panizza's mother hid and moved her children from house to house or city to city to avoid the infringement of church and state in the private domain of the family. It was her fanaticism which instilled in Panizza a lasting hatred of Catholicism and state institutions as well as a deep love for the Lutheran tradition of rebellion, which he idealized and eventually transformed into iconoclasm.

By the time he began his university studies in 1877, Panizza already showed signs that he would not fit into proper German society. He had not been able to finish his studies at the Gymnasium, had wandered from job to job, and reacted extremely sensitively to any kind of constraint. Moreover, he became attracted to Bohemian life, especially in Munich. Sometime between 1877 and 1880 Panizza, who liked to associate with prostitutes,[5] contracted syphillis, which probably contributed to his eventual derangement. His interest in deviation and insanity—several relatives had gone insane—as well as his own proclivities led him to concentrate on genetics, mental diseases, and psychology while at the university. Though there were no traces yet of a pathological obsession, Panizza was clearly intrigued by abnormality and sought a clinical and moral understanding of degeneration.

After Panizza received his degree as a doctor of medicine in 1880, his first position was ironically in a Munich clinic for the insane, where he would find himself as a patient many years later. His involvement in the profession was short-lived; by 1885 he discovered that writing poetry was a therapeutic way of dealing with the deep psychological problems that plagued him. Almost all his poems in his early volumes *Düstere Lieder* (1886) and *Londoner Lieder* (1887) express a disdain for the philistine life and a morbid interest in gothic motifs and death. Panizza sought to project his "warped and crazy" ideas on paper to preserve himself and also to pursue fame.[6] But preservation based on a warped frame of mind was bound to lead to catastrophe.

From 1890 to 1894, when Panizza wrote some of his best critical essays and stories, it appeared that he might develop into one of the more gifted "anti-bourgeois" writers gathered around Munich's avant-garde journal *Die Gesellschaft*. But Panizza overstepped the limits of decorum and tolerance as far as the Catholic Church was concerned when he published his notorious drama *Das Liebeskonzil* (*The Council of Love*) in 1894. Panizza set his play in 1495 when the Church under Pope Alexander was scandalously corrupt. God, a senile, impotent old man, holds council with the pretty, vain Maria and the anemic, gullible Jesus to decide how they should punish the sinful ways of the Pope and his followers. By the end of the drama, Panizza demonstrated that the origins of syphilis on earth could be traced to God and Maria, who give their holy blessings to the actions of the devil.

Naturally, this play was banned by the censors and confiscated by the police. Panizza was accused of blasphemy by the state authorities. Although he might have avoided a trial, he appeared to desire publicity because of his ambitions as a writer; moreover, he could not imagine that he would be severely punished. After a court hearing in the spring of 1895, Panizza was sentenced to one year imprisonment by a Munich judge. The trial and sentence caused a great sensation, even disbelief among intellectuals. Panizza became a *cause célèbre*; however, he received more notoriety than he had bargained for. Moreover, the prison experience seemed to shatter him while making him more conscious about the way social conditions operate politically on individuals.

What is interesting about this period of Panizza's life is that the sicker he became, the more politically he reacted. His fascination with his own case of syphilis had led him to write an outlandish drama that attacked the church for ultimately causing his own degeneration. By acting out his own sickness in public, he offended the public sense of morality and was obliged to experience the social consequences firsthand—in mind and body.

After his prison experience, Panizza went through steadily increasing phases of deterioration. He left Munich in 1896, continued to write vitriolic attacks on Germany, was forced to leave Zurich in 1898 after a criminal charge involving a minor as prostitute. Finally making his home in Paris, he felt that he was continually being hounded by German detectives. In 1901 he returned to Munich, where he was arrested for libel against the state and then declared mentally unfit to stand trial.

Abandoned by his family and most of his friends, Panizza once again travelled to Paris, but he could no longer write or live calmly because of hallucinations and whistling noises in his head. By 1904 Panizza realized that he could not continue living without institutional help, and he returned to Bavaria, the state he hated most. In 1905 he was declared incapable of discharging his own affairs and sent to an asylum near Bayreuth, where he spent the next sixteen years of his life. He associated mainly with other patients who were hopelessly sick, wrote journals which became a multilingual amalgamation of the Bible, mythology, pornography, philosophy, and vituperation, and in the end was totally unable to comprehend the events of the world around him. On September 28, 1921, he died from a heart attack.

In 1897, while living in Switzerland, Panizza wrote a diatribe in a work entitled *Dialogue im Geiste Huttens* (*Dialogues in the Spirit of Hutten*), which is revealing as a kind of epitaph, especially since Ulrich von Hutten, Panizza's guiding spirit, was a humanist poet, who fought against the ecclesiastical princes and died in exile.

Optimist

And this is your prognosis for Germans? Have you abandoned hope? Don't you believe that there will be men in our time who will rise up and sweep away the masses with them? I'll admit that the masses in Germany are difficult to move. They are like asphalt. But asphalt burns. Think of people like Hus, Luther, Kant, Lassalle . . .

Pessimist

Yes, but they were half crazy. That was the good thing about them. Psychiatrists declared Luther insane. He had hallucinations and threw an inkstand at the devil. The others also had their symptoms. Kant declared that he could not say everything he thought. It's the same with all these people. A German can only achieve the highest at the very moment he becomes mentally deranged, and this is followed by incarceration in an insane asylum or death on a scaffold. Luther was most fortunate. Anyway it was more propitious to live in those early times when there were many small principalities, for this allowed one to express oneself more freely than today. You could run from one sovereign to the next for protection. Someone like Schubart would write a satire about the mistress of his majesty. Then he had to flee and run to the next state to Prince B. The latter received him with open arms, gave him something to eat, and he was allowed to—like Schiller—write a new drama about Prince A. Then he would fall in disgrace, flee again, run to Prince C. Here again he would rub his hands, receive something to eat—perhaps even, like Hutten, the poet's laurels—and he would write a new *Dialogue* or a *Trias Romana* against the Pope, Kaiser, or Prince B. This was the way one stirred up thirty-six potentates—and genius triumphed.

Optimist

Hold it! Hold it! What are you saying? My God! Is this a history of literature or a history of the Reformation?. . . .

Pessimist

Well, was it any different with Luther? One day he begged and sang in front of the windows of the rich. The next day he nailed theses on the church door. The day after he was ripped apart by students. He was thrown back and forth between the Diet of

Worms, Wartburg, the legates, his prince, the Kaiser, the Pope and his order, tormented and banned, and so he reeled, swindled, and shirked his way, so to speak, through all these circumstances—one day he consented to bigamy, the next day he anathematized the peasants—and, after he was thrown back and forth by his anger and visions and ignited the tough masses of asphalt, he was actually buried without losing his head.

Optimist
My God?! —Lord almighty! —Those were difficult times. — But he survived —Why can't one survive like that today?

Pessimist
Today?! —Today, if one expresses a free thought, there are only three ways open to him: the insane asylum, prison, or flight. If he declares himself mentally disturbed, then the district doctor closes one eye and—he disappears. If he is stubborn and insists that he is sane, then the courts take charge and—he disappears. If he leaves the land of asphalt before things become too hot, then the barriers close behind him and—he disappears.[7]

These reflections along with other writings completed after his prison experience indicate to what extent Panizza used his paranoia to grasp the underlying motives of German society's operative rational principles. Unfortunately, Panizza rarely questioned his own motives and failed to find a modus vivendi for elaborating his criticisms of society without becoming self-destructive. Perhaps, one could argue, his obsession with church and state was not of his own making. Yet, his vituperative spirit and ambition to become an iconoclast contributed greatly to his persecution complex. It was as though he acted in extreme complicity with the state and decided subconsciously, at one point, to prevent any kind of social reconciliation. His own mind became the prisonhouse of his world. He became the victim as victimizer. It was from this vantage point that he sought to understand German society, and it is clear that throughout his life his sickness made him into a disturbing critic of intolerable social conditions that German institutions claimed were satisfactory and tolerable.

Panizza's *The Operated Jew* was written at a time when he was still in possession of his mind but had already manifested clear signs of mental disturbance and was deeply perturbed about various developments in Germany. This personal and social configuration of disturbance helps explain his need to portray the symbiotic relationship between Germans and Jews. But, before analyzing the significance of Panizza's portrayal of the Jew in relation to anti-Semitism, assimilation, and the manner in which Germans operated on themselves as Jews at the end of the nineteenth century, we must discuss his intentions in writing the story. Why did he choose the negative stereotype of the Jew to work through problems he himself was experiencing in Germany? What drew him to the Jew and other minority figures, and why was he so disparaging of these types, along with the model German citizens?

Given the limited biographical information we have about Panizza, it is not easy to answer these questions. However, one fact that we can be sure about is the matter of his anti-Semitism. About this time Panizza wrote one other story, *Der Goldenregen* (*The Bow of Gold*), and two essays, *Prolegomena zum Preisausschreiben: Verbesserung unserer Rasse* (*Prologomena to the Contest: Improvement of Our Race*) and *Die "unsittlichen Gebrüder Grimm und die neue "Sittlichkeit" jüdisch-deutscher Verlagsbuchhändler* (*The "Immoral" Brothers Grimm and the New "Morality" of Jewish-German Publishers' Bookdealers*), all of which depicted Jews as materialistic, greedy, dark, squat, and ugly. He clearly viewed Jews in a traditional anti-Semitic fashion.

At the same time, he admired Jews for their intellectual prowess and mercantile talents. Jews were a race he disliked, but he did not campaign to have them liquidated or improved. Like many liberal intellectuals of his day[8] who associated with assimilated Jews and still shared common prejudices against them and their kind, he never tried to understand why he had such prejudicial notions. He simply equated Jews with moneylenders and capitalists and described them as small, dark, swarthy, and ugly— threatening in a sensual way, which is why they had to be ridiculed. In sum, he resented Jews, whom he hardly knew and did not understand, and bought all the clichés as sociological and natural givens. Yet when Panizza sought to vent his anger against German institutions, Jews were used in an ambivalent way. While directing most of his vindictiveness against the Catholic Church, the state, and modern German citizens, Panizza would identify subconsciously with Jews and other outcast groups—as though he could never abandon that side of humanity, no matter how decrepit, to the authoritarian institutions which threatened to instrumentalize every aspect of life for the sake of order. Even when his anti-Semitism was changed into philo-Semitism after his prison experiences of 1895–96,[9] it did not mean that he became a champion of Jews, but that he realized more consciously how much his own suffering was related to the way Jews were being treated. The Jew, Panizza perceived, was part of himself.

To say the least, Panizza's anti-Semitism was peculiar even though it was rooted in deeply traditional hates and fears shared by other Germans of his time. Like his "Aryan compatriots," he witnessed and was influenced by the heated debate over the Jewish question during the Wilhelmian period, but his views did not correspond to any of the standard positions. He took sides in his own inimitable fashion—against both the Jews and the German racists. Panizza drew upon a socially acceptable anti-

Semitic tradition in literature for his caricatures and exaggerated the stereotype in order to be provocative.[10] As model for Faitel Stern, Panizza recalled characters from Friedrich Freiherr von Holzschuher's parody, *Die Manzipaziuhn der houchloebliche kienigliche bayrische Juedenschaft. (The Emancipation of the Praise-worthy Royal Bavarian Jewish Community.) En Edress an die houchverehrliche Herren Lanstaend, ousgestodiert vun Itzig Feitel Stern (An Address to the Honorable Gentlemen of the Parliament, Delivered by Itzig Feitel Stern.)* (1834)[11] and Gustav Freytag's best-selling novel, *Soll und Haben* (1855) *(Debit and Credit).*[12] Holzschuher wrote under the pseudonym of Itzig Faitel Stern, using a comical German Yiddish to parody the efforts of Jews to attain assimilation. Freytag employed the figure of Veitel Itzig to demonstrate the exploitative tendencies of rich Jewish businessmen. Holzschuher was an avowed anti-Semite who thought that Jews could never be fully assimilated into German society. Freytag was a liberal who condemned usury and associated Jews with some of the worst aspects of capitalism, but he felt that they could be improved by becoming full-blooded Germans. Panizza harked back to Holzschuher and Freytag, but he was not inclined to treat the Jewish question specifically without raising the matter of how Germans operated in general, nor did he care whether he would be considered anti-Semitic. By 1893, he had attacked almost all established schools of thought, religions, and political parties, and took pride mainly in the fact that he was considered an iconoclast. This is not to dismiss his disdain of Jews, but to explore the complex nature of Panizza's depiction of Jews: the operated Jew, Faitel Stern, was both an indicator of Panizza's anti-Semitism and a literary device meant to articulate his critical notions of eugenics and to explore his own inability to adapt to German society.

In 1893, the same year that he wrote *The Operated Jew*, Panizza published his remarkable essay *Prolegomena to the Con-*

test: Improvement of Our Race. This article appeared in *Die Gesellschaft*[13] and actually criticized the journal for holding a contest and awarding a prize to the best essay on the topic "Can One Improve the Human Race?" As a doctor thoroughly familiar with the eugenic experiments and operations of that time,[14] Panizza took the position that each step made toward improving the human race would mean a curtailment of individual freedom. He feared that anyone with a slight disorder or disease might be prevented by the state and medical authorities from marrying, procreating, or living the way he or she wanted.

Since the ideas in this essay are linked to the intentions and basic notions of *The Operated Jew*, I want to deal briefly with its major points. Panizza claims that, since the question concerning the improvement of the race was raised primarily with physical fitness as focus, it implied that an improved mind was dependent on an improved physical body. He refutes this premise by arguing that 1) numerous superb physical specimens from the country fail to meet the demands of urban life and fall apart; 2) great leaders, artists and thinkers like Caesar, Napoleon, Pascal, Voltaire, Frederick the Great, Byron, and Richard Wagner all had small, crippled or diseased bodies; 3) even the Jews, despite their physical decrepitude, have developed better minds (especially mercantile Jews) so that the German race cannot keep pace with them. Panizza seeks to demonstrate that the question of improvement really implies the elimination of what state and society designate as pernicious elements. Yet, he maintains that it is difficult to get rid of various diseases such as typhoid, tuberculosis, and syphillis, and that such harmful agents as nicotine, coffee, absinthe, morphine, and alcohol have proven stimulating for cultural work. Moreover, mental diseases and consumption have made numerous talented individuals more aware and sensitive. Panizza asserts that it is almost impossible to control and supervise disease and addiction because the state itself is composed of human beings, all who have their weak-nesses and disorders. Historically it may have been easier to control the spread of diseases and derangement through the arbitrary commands of rulers and ruling groups. Thus, certain people were castrated, sterilized, ostracized, or annihilated. However, Panizza remarks that the Enlightenment humanely changed the situation by recognizing the natural rights of individ-uals and calling for the protection of minority groups—whether they be misfits, unusual types, or carriers of diseases. Ultimately, he claims that

> our race has not at all become "worse." In its cerebral achieve-ments it has made immense progress. These achievements are our highest triumph. We don't want to live without them any longer. On the other hand, our physical and especially our vegetative achievements appear indeed to have become worse. We must chew rhubarb, swallow quinine, and help build up our blood through iron. Our sensory organs, especially our smell and sight, are not as advanced as those of the accomplished Indians and Negroes. And our age expectancy seems to have been reduced. — However, in the short span of time, our ability to enjoy has increased threefold in comparison with the past. —And, for sure, to enjoy is to live![15]

Panizza's essay is filled with jabs at German racist beliefs such as "the blood and iron" notions of Bismarck and at fashionable health trends such as the consumption of rhubarb and quinine. This criticism is related to his deep hatred of the state and institutionalized modes of surveillance and control. Moreover, as someone stricken with syphillis and with a history of mental disease in his family, Panizza opposed eugenic experimentation and Darwinist theories of improving the human race by op-erating on and controlling human beings.

Panizza's personal concern about eugenics and his opposition to medical experiments on humans is important to understand because these attitudes are connected to the contradictory way he related to Jews, blacks, Indians, and other minority groups. While belittling certain characteristics of these types, he took a firm stand against those legal measures aimed at supervising the disenfranchised and aliens in German society. We know that Panizza often used his writing psychologically as therapy, and in *The Operated Jew* it is clear that Panizza is not to be identified solely with the narrator, but rather with both the German commentator and the Jewish protagonist. The operating German becomes the operated Jew in more ways than one: Panizza takes an ironic stance by portraying himself in the form of a Jew. There is something schizophrenic in the relationship between the first-person narrator and the third-person object Faitel Stern: two sides of the same individual, one dissecting in a detached and ruthless way the passive compliance of the diseased and malformed subject, who eventually destroys himself by seeking to conform to the normative Aryan standards of German society. Yet it is not only self-hate which makes the psychological components of this story so compelling, but the manner in which Panizza also derives pleasure by mocking German nationalism and the standard norms and customs of respectable German society while making a fiasco out of the eugenic operations of German scientists, who dehumanize individuals with their alleged progressive and enlightened experiments.[16] Ultimately, Faitel's failure to become a German is a virtue; or rather, humankind's resistance to the instrumentalized treatment of a human being which was becoming more and more prevalent in German society is depicted as a triumph of "weak humanity" over "strong scientific power" aiming to perfect the human race. To be sure, Panizza's general hatred of the German state and institutionalized science leads to a dubious victory over his self-hatred. As operated German, the operated Jew is a wreck at the end. Only in being exterminated does this figure offer a scintillating personal comment on racism, science, and the servile, hypocritical behavior of respectable citizens in Germany. But *The Operated Jew* is more than just a personal comment. It is also a cultural document that sheds light on two social factors which need more elaboration: the socio-psychopathological tendency of the Germans and the political transformation of anti-Semitism which brought about an identity crisis for German-Jews.

Perhaps the best-known discussion of the collective psychopathology of the Germans is Norman Cohn's *Warrant for Genocide*.[17] He advanced the hypothesis that notions of one form or another about the Jewish world conspiracy were "above all a matter of unconscious negative projections, i.e. of the mental mechanism by which human beings read into the behavior of others the anarchic tendencies which they fear to recognize in themselves. More specifically . . . in this form of anti-Semitism the Jews, as a collectivity, are unconsciously seen both as the 'bad' son, i.e., the rebellious son full of murderous wishes toward the father, and the 'bad' father, i.e., the potential torturer, castrator, and killer of the son" (256–57). In other words, the Jew is a necessary symbiotic part of the pathological anti-Semitic personality. In order to feel safe, the pathological anti-Semite must eventually kill or control that side of him/her which cannot be accepted. As Cohn points out, "it is a phenomenon which only begins to make sense when one recalls that a paranoiac murderer too can feel terrified of his harmless victims. For what these people see as the enemy is in fact the destructiveness and cruelty in their own psyches, externalized. And the greater the unconscious sense of guilt, the more fearsome the imaginary enemy" (265–66).

Though Panizza did not consciously endeavor to dissect the paranoiac form of schizophrenia as mass delusion or as peculiar to Germans, he subconsciously depicted a paradigm of the clinical syndrome in *The Operated Jew* that reflected strong German prejudices toward Jews. On one level, Panizza captures the manner in which Germans are socialized to police and punish themselves for expressing dissent: the two sides of the problem represented by the narrator and Faitel Stern displays this schizophrenic situation. The ugly Jew, symbolic of aggressive and sensual urges, must be either controlled or exterminated by the narrator. Thus, while the narrator projects certain unacceptable fantasies onto the Jew, he eliminates them by eliminating the Jew. On a larger social level, Panizza shows how all the German characters who partake in this experiment are carried away by the desire to cleanse their race of an ugly smear—to create the perfect Aryan. Moreover, almost all the Germans portrayed by Panizza live under the spell of a delusion that there is such a thing as a pure Aryan soul and that Jews besmirch this soul. Such "demented conditions" set the scene for the acceptable Jew-killing. What is striking about Panizza's portrayal of how the Germans operate on Faitel Stern is their composed collaboration. Again Cohn is helpful for suggesting how Panizza went beyond his own personal paranoia to illuminate a collective pathology: "though the individuals who made up a group of Jew-killers are well within the bounds of reality, and most of them are not even fanatics, and even the fanatics are far from mad—yet it is perfectly true that the group as a whole behaves like a paranoiac in the grip of his delusion" (265). The Jew, as the German narrator and characters perceive him, is one of their own making and, deluded by their fears and drives, they operate on the Jew to control themselves.

The psychic play and patterns in *The Operated Jew* become more clear when they are related to the political transformation of anti-Semitism and the identity crisis of German Jews. Again, though not his intention, Panizza was able to reflect upon a socio-psychological crisis that was to have a bearing on the future development of Germany. As Werner Jochmann has asserted, "the Jewish question along with the German question had clearly become a matter of politics"[18] during the Wilhelminian period, and numerous historians consider the shift in the framing of the Jewish question as pivotal for explaining certain trends leading to the rise of German fascism and the eventual destruction of European Jewry.

The push toward emancipation and assimilation did not contribute to greater acceptance of Jews when the German nation was founded in 1871, but to a new form of racist and political anti-Semitic segregation and definition of Jewishness. As Reinhard Rürup has so aptly demonstrated, the advent of capitalist industrialization with improved technological control for increased production, the growth of nationalist and racist thinking and the effects of urbanization on an agrarian population qualified the conditions of acceptance and assimilation for Jews after 1870.[19] Moreover, an economic crisis during the 1870s led to a state and church campaign against Jews, who functioned as scapegoats and were held responsible for the decline in traditional German virtues and customs, as well as general socioeconomic decline. Jews gradually became the measure for everything that was un-German. This calculated structural shift in the policy of church and state sought to influence social ideas and behavior.

The quest for national identity, a pure race, and a genuine German soul was at the heart of the *Kulturkampf*,[20] which was essentially fought to solidify and legitimate the new hegemonic formation of Junker-industrial elites. The uprooting of local customs, sacrifices of regional autonomy, and increase in political and technological control literally over the bodies of the citizens in the socialization process left huge nonsynchronous gaps among Germans of different social groups and caused immense social anxiety.[21] One of the means of social control was to create a sense of superiority among Christian Germans while pointing a finger at the inferior Jews, who were allegedly seeking to contaminate the German race and undermine social stability. The power of the Jews supposedly rested on money and intrigue, but they could never wrest away the German soul from true-blooded Aryans. Despite the legal recognition and high degree of assimilation of Jews by the 1870s and 1880s, they could never become *real* Germans. Their structural importance with the rise of the nation-state and capitalist economy demanded that they remain foreign elements, pernicious agents, the embodiment of disease. German identity depended on the distortion of Jewish identity and thus was a distortion in itself. As George Mosse has clearly demonstrated

> Germans searched for a uniqueness to distinguish themselves from aspects of modernity they disliked. They wished to draw out of their personality and national heritage new forms and insights whose validity could be proved by their relationship to an external, cosmological entity. Consequently, since they rejected all mechanization and industrialization, they ascribed intellectual and "oriental" qualities to the people who had supposedly forced modernity upon the Germans—the Jews.[22]

For Jews, too, an identity crisis had developed that had begun in the late eighteenth century but had become magnified with greater possibilities for assimilation and emancipation in the nineteenth century.[23] The quest to be accepted as German and Jew (articulated so admirably by Jakob Wassermann in his book *My Life as German and Jew*)[24] remained integral to the Jewish struggle for *real* acceptance. However, the impossibility for such real acceptance in the Wilhelminian period, even after legal recognition of equal rights, led many assimilated Jews to distance themselves from the Jewish tradition, to self-hate, and to a particular hostility toward the East European Jews, who came to settle in Germany.[25] In other words, the operative force of German anti-Semitism undermined the confidence and identity of German Jews, who were gradually driven to function in the role assigned to them the more they sought to become good German bourgeois citizens. This middle-class proclivity of German Jews made them all the more associated with capitalism, internationalism, and cosmopolitanism.[26] Thus, as they took advantage of emancipation, they were able to assimilate within German society but not on their own terms. In reality, Jews were forced to walk a one-way street of self-denial while functioning as aliens and scapegoats in the German socio-economic framework that had become infused with racist and enlightened ideas to improve the Aryan/Christian stock.

Though it is clear that Panizza did not purport to portray the quandary of assimilated German Jews, his deep concern with eugenics and social control led him indirectly to measure the value of assimilation for Jews in anti-Semitic Germany. Faitel's overwhelming passion to appear German and possess a German soul leads ironically to his destruction. In Wilhelminian society, to be German meant for a Jew self-destruction. Each step in this negative assimilatory process is described with a clinical eye in painful, grotesque detail. The narrative manner of the tale is reminiscent of Kafka's distanced, almost scientific toying with his protagonists as they seek acceptance and identification while literally being operated on in an excruciating manner and eventually being destroyed. But there is a significant difference between Kafka and Panizza arising from their antithetical views on Jews and assimilation. Kafka sympathized greatly with his helplessly confused heroes who often deceived themselves because they wanted to belong to a world which treated them with indifference if not hate. Panizza expresses little sympathy for his protagonist in *The Operated Jew*. He has a scrutinizing medical student, ostensibly Faitel Stern's best friend, first assemble the Jew before our eyes, then gradually operate on him, and finally dissect him in a crude, fantastical manner. The impossibility of such a process makes it seem all the more possible. Panizza exaggerates and uses caricatures, but his starting point is a close observation of Wilhelminian society. Each step Faitel Stern takes to control and eliminate his Jewishness is laughable, not so much because his obvious stereotypical Jewish traits are ridiculous, but because the German qualities, which he wants to adapt, are preposterous. To become a blond, blue-eyed German stalwart means learning how to walk stiffly, utter pretentious phrases, dispense with critical thinking, and to pander to money, power, and the upper classes. In a way it is a credit to Faitel Stern's Jewish "essence"— his rebellious nature—that he cannot become German, that the experiment fails, and that weak human flesh proves stronger than a eugenic operation.

The terrifying image at the end of Panizza's tale—Faitel as a human wreck—is an uncanny anticipation of German annihilation of Jews during the Nazi period. Perhaps it is because he felt so intensely that Germans were operating on him, that Panizza was able to identify with the Jewish condition. This fantastic projection, a vivid condemnation of Germans and Jews alike, is the product of a disturbed German writer in the process of becoming acutely paranoid. Ironically, it was because of his derangement that Panizza, himself both a medical doctor and creative artist, could place his finger on operative processes in Germany that were preventing autonomous development of individuality. These processes did not abate in his own time and have not abated after two world wars. The German as operated Jew remains in both Germanies today, despite the fact that little trace remains either of Jews themselves or of what they wanted to realize in their struggle for emancipation and acceptance.

Notes

1. "Oskar Panizza" in *Gesammelte Werke*, Vol. I (Reinbek bei Hamburg: Rowohlt, 1960): 696–97.

2. "E.T.A. Hoffmann und Oskar Panizza" in *Gesammelte Werke*, Vol. II (Frankfurt am Main: Suhrkamp, 1977): 648.

3. Two writers who played an important part in Panizza's rediscovery after World War II are Jean Brejoux and Hans Prescher. Brejoux translated *Das Liebeskonzil* as *Le Concile d'Amour* (Paris, 1960). André Breton wrote the preface to this volume, and Brejoux added an afterword which includes biographical material. Prescher edited *Das Liebeskonzil und andere Schriften* (Neuwied: Luchterhand, 1964) and wrote a significant afterword in praise of Panizza.

4. The other two most significant studies of Panizza are Peter D. G. Brown's *Oskar Panizza: His Life and Works* (New York: Peter Lang, 1983) and Michael Bauer, *Oskar Panizza: Ein literarisches Porträt* (Munich: Carl Hanser, 1984). In addition to these studies, my remarks in this section are based on Friedrich Lippert, ed. *In Memoriam Oskar Panizza* (Munich, 1926), which includes important autobiographical material and statements by Panizza's mother and his guardian Lippert; Friedrich Wilhelm Kantzenbach, "Der Dichter Oskar Panizza und der Pfarrer Friedrich Lippert, eine Lebensbegegnung," *Zeitschrift für Religions-und Geistesgeschichte* 26 (1974): 125–42; Otto Julius Bierbaum, "Oskar Panizza," *Die Gesellschaft* 9 (1893): 978–84; and a general reading of Panizza's writings including the articles which appeared in *Die Gesellschaft* and in the *Zürcher Diskußionen*.

5. Panizza even wrote a fascinating defense of prostitutes. See "Prostitution. Eine Gegenwartsstudie," *Die Gesellschaft* 8 (1892): 1159–83.

6. See Peter D. G. Brown, "Oskar Panizza's First and Last Books: A Study in Late Nineteenth-Century Poetry," *The Germanic Review* XLVIII (November 1973): 269–87.

7. *Dialoge im Geiste Huttens* (Zurich: Zürcher Diskußionen, 1897): 16–20.

8. See Alfred D. Low, *Jews in the Eyes of the Germans: From the Enlighten-*

ment to Imperial Germany (Philadelphia: Institute for the Study of Human Issues, 1979): 359–409.

9. The change is noticeable in *Dialoge im Geiste Huttens*, p. 38: "We are like the Jews. They were slave laborers first under the Egyptians. Later they became the prisoners of the Babylonians. Then they were the vassals of the Romans. And today their homeland belongs to the Turks. But their spirit, their *esprit*, their instinct has conquered the world. And their monotheism is one of the most powerful spiritual forces that has ever been of service to humankind." See also "Intra muros et extra," *Zürcher Diskußionen*, II, 2021 (1899): 14.

10. See Roy Pascal's discussion "The Jew as Alien and Bourgeois" in *From Naturalism to Expressionism* (New York: Barnes and Noble, 1973): 67–84, and Hans Mayer's "Jüdische Kunstfiguren im bürgerlichen Roman" in *Außenseiter* (Frankfurt am Main: Suhrkamp, 1975): 381–413.

11. For a discussion of Holzschuher's significance, see Jacob Katz, *Emancipation and Assimilation* (Westmead, England: Farnborough, Gregg, 1972): 37–39.

12. For remarks about Freytag's significance, see Ernest K. Bramsted, *Aristocracy and the Middle-Classes in Germany* (Chicago: University of Chicago Press, 1964): 132–49.

13. 9 (1893): 275–89.

14. Cf. Stephen L. Chorover, *From Genesis to Genocide: The Meaning of Human Nature and the Power of Behavioral Control* (Cambridge: MIT Press, 1979): 80–81. "The Nazi extermination program was a logical extermination of sociobiological ideas and eugenics doctrines which had nothing specifically to do with Jews and which flourished widely in Germany well before the era of Third Reich."

15. "*Prolegomena zum Preisausschreiben*," 289.

16. The consequences of such racist experiments are depicted in Alexander Kluge's chilling story "Ein Liebesversuch" in *Lebensläufe* (Stuttgart: Goverts Verlag, 1962). This story was translated by Leila Vennewitz as "An Experiment in Love" in *Case Histories* (New York: Holmes & Meier, 1988). For a significant discussion of this text, see Leo Finndegen's "Kommentar," *Freibeuter* I (1979): 90–93.

17. New York: Harper & Row, 1967. Subsequent citations appear in the text.

18. "Struktur und Funktion des deutschen Antisemitismus," *Juden im Wilhelminischen Deutschland 1890–1914*, ed. Werner E. Mosse (Tübingen: Mohr, 1976): 396.

19. "Emanzipation und Krise—Zur Geschichte der 'Judenfrage' in Deutschland vor 1890" in *Juden im Wilhelminischen Reich 1890–1914*, ed. Werner E. Mosse (Tübingen: Mohr, 1976): 1–56. See also Reinhard Rürup, *Emanzipation und Antisemitismus* (Göttingen: Vandenhoecke, Ruprecht, 1975).

20. See Uriel Tal, *Christians and Jews in Germany* (Ithaca: Cornell University Press, 1975) and Pochmann, "Struktur und Funktion des Antisemitismus," 389–478.

21. See Michel Foucault's significant work on this subject, *Discipline and Punish* (New York: Pantheon, 1979). Panizza's life and works are related to Foucault's study of how institutional processes operate on the body and mind to form passive and complying citizens.

22. *The Crisis of German Ideology* (New York: Grosset & Dunlap, 1964): 58.

23. See Robert Weltsch, "Die schleichende Krise der jüdischen Identität" in Mosse, 689–704.

24. English edition, New York, 1933. German edition, *Mein Weg als Deutscher und Jude* (Berlin: S. Fischer, 1921).

25. Cf. Theodor Lessing, *Jüdischer Selbstaß* (Berlin: Jüdischer Verlag, 1930) and Hans Mayer, "Jüdischer Selbsthaß" in *Außenseiter*, 414–21.

26. Rürup, "Emanzipation und Krise—Zur Geschichte der 'Judenfrage' in Deutschland vor 1890," 27–41.

Salomo Friedlaender: The Anonymous Jew as Laughing Philosopher

After he fled from the Nazis in 1933, Salomo Friedlaender settled in Paris, where he published his last book of grotesque tales entitled *The Laughing Job* under his customary pseudonym Mynona, an anagram in German for *Anonym* or "Anonymous."[1] This slim volume contained an introductory poem and two stories, "Magical Revolution: Utopia" and "The Laughing Job," which were surprisingly optimistic in a macabre sense. In particular, "The Laughing Job" deserves special attention because it contains the core of Friedlaender's mystical neo-Kantian philosophy and indicates how he sought to create an ethical figure for Jews and Germans alike that would serve as a model for transcending the negative German-Jewish symbiosis of his times.

In "The Laughing Job," Joshua Zander, a rich Jewish owner of a mining company, is confronted with a series of mishaps. Even though he shows support for his workers during a period of hard times and strikes and refuses to be compromised by either the fascists or socialists, he is finally overcome by a powerful wave of anti-Semitism produced by the state.

A principle was mendaciously created out of the common vulgar anti-Semitism, and all the civil servants were obliged to accept this principle as their duty. The entire culture became barbaric. . . . Joshua and the others of his religious faith were fallaciously degraded and made into pariahs so that the masses were won over this way. Moreover, lunatics were now produced, and among them were all the so-called "educated people." They bred a spiritual plague that was much more dangerous than the plagues of the Middle Ages. And finally they used this also to infect Joshua's workers. (53)

The result was that the workers abandon him; his wife and children join the Communist Party and then flee the country; his property is confiscated, and he is arrested and taken to a concentration camp.

Since Joshua's victimizers suspect that he has hidden a great deal of money and treasures, they do not kill him. Instead they interrogate and torture him with the hope that he will reveal where he has concealed everything. Joshua, on the other hand, had never believed that his money would guarantee him happiness; rather he had always counted on inner moral principles to make himself worthy of happiness. Therefore, when General Göbbelring threatens him with bodily harm, he can only laugh, and he continues to laugh each time the General increases the threat of torture. In fact, Joshua makes a fool out of the General by denying that his body is identical with the person called Joshua Zander. Infuriated, the General orders him to be whipped a hundred times, and again Joshua replies: "The body becomes a corpse when you free it from the spirit. But do you know for sure whether you're not freeing the spirit by doing this?" (55).

Beaten within an inch of his life, Joshua is advised by a well-meaning doctor not to irritate the General anymore. However, Joshua replies that his spirit has magical powers and will actually gain the upper hand through all the corporeal mistreatment because it will not succumb to brute force. Left alone, Joshua begins whispering: "This body of mine is only outside. It is not me myself. That is indeed the miraculous truth, which gives me the strength to see through all these deceptions and to enjoy my bodily sufferings like an impartial observer. I have this strength. But who am I? It is only through my I that my flesh lives, and I am a mystery, a mystery, that I want to reveal!" (57).

To reveal himself, Joshua hangs himself with bed sheets. However, he survives his body, and when the General returns to his cell, he still mistakes Joshua's body for Zander. He threatens to mutilate him, but Joshua takes the knife of a guard and sticks it into his own heart. Soon he sprouts wings and floats above the General, who runs frightened from the room. At this point Joshua explains to the doctor that his spirit is not only immortal but it can also infuse a body with life to show how immortal it is. "Resurrection through death. I no longer make a distinction between self-trust and trust in God and have liberated the laws of my self, my spirit, my reason so radically from all the laws of nature that the laws of nature obey the law of my spirit" (60).

Before the doctor can reply to Joshua, the General returns with some troops, shoots the angelic body of Joshua, and has it burned. But Joshua once again rises from the ashes as an angel and announces to the General that the time has come for the domination of the spirit over all brutality and racism. He touches the General with one of his wings and transforms him and his followers into creatures that resemble pets. Then he orders them to capture their leader, called the *Führer*. Once this is accomplished, Joshua transforms the *Führer* into a puppet and frees all prisoners providing them with the opportunity to become *Vernunftmenschen*, or men of reason. That is, they are to recognize that their spirit of freedom depends on their own reason, which laughingly liberates them from the laws of nature. While the *Führer* is conducted to an insane asylum, Joshua continues to teach all people how they can free themselves from nature through their reason.

Given conditions in Europe in 1935, it is certainly possible to read this bizarre tale as wishful thinking on the part of a German-Jewish writer turned somewhat demented in his Paris exile. As grotesque and almost obscene as his optimism seems in this story, however, it was not really unusual for Friedlaender, and he certainly was not insane when he wrote it. In fact, his tale was part of a serious philosophical program that he had conceived over a period of twenty-five years. He intended his grotesque narratives to illustrate what theory was unable to accomplish, but what he himself was able more or less to accomplish in real life. In this regard, "The Laughing Job" offered greater possibilities of overcoming anti-Semitism and problems of Jewish identity than his earlier tale "The Operated Goy" (1922). By making Joshua a universal categorical imperative, Friedlaender wanted to demonstrate how the anonymous Jew can survive and how he himself survived. Yet, one must still ask the question whether Friedlaender was serious or delirious. Did he really think in 1935 that his life, the life of the laughing Job, could serve as an example for those who read his words? Did he really think Kantian ethics and what he called "creative indifference" was the answer to Hitler and anti-Semitism? To answer these questions we must recapitulate a life that he paradoxically wanted to keep anonymous by adhering to a most unique and challenging philosophy.

Though Friedlaender actually wrote an autobiography at one point in his life, he did not make it easy for later biographers:[2] He purposely eliminated and concealed dates and exact references in his writings because he did not want his life to seem either monumental or singular. If it was to be considered exemplary, he thought, then it should be because of its spiritual quality. Therefore, his autobiography was to serve a universal principle in the same manner that Kant's philosophy sought to propose universal standards of ethics and morals. Though this viewpoint may seem arrogant, Friedlaender was more obsessed than arrogant, more devoted to his mystical and philosophical musings than insistent on achieving fame and imposing his will on his readers.

Born on May 4, 1871 in a small town called Gollantsch near Posen in the eastern tip of the newly formed Wilhelminian Empire, Friedlaender was the eldest son of a Jewish doctor and a musically inclined mother, herself a gifted singer and pianist. His attachment to both parents was very strong but riddled with conflict. They provided him with the best possible opportunities to develop himself, and he, in turn, did not use these opportunities according to their high expectations. As he states in his *Autobiography*: "In this bourgeois home we breathed the aroma of the classics in literature and music. Melodies and poems came flying at me. I liked to recite and studied the violin."[3] But, Friedlaender was also spoiled and stubborn; he only took his school lessons seriously when he was interested in the subject matter. Because he suffered from bronchial diseases and was often sick, Friedlaender's father hired private tutors to educate him and also sent him to private schools. Yet he was not an obliging student and resisted any kind of discipline. Indicative of his rebellious nature during his youth was his inclination to read a great deal of fantasy—the works of Jules Verne, the *Arabian Nights*, and fairy tales—works counter to the traditional classical canon he was supposed to learn to absorb. Later in his life these fantastic tales would serve as the basis for many of his own grotesque works.

By 1885, his father, a severe taskmaster, sent Friedlaender to Berlin, where he was placed under the supervision of a sister-in-law to see if the Prussian educational system might lead Friedlaender to gain some respect for authority. Yet, when he returned to Posen in 1887, the experiment was declared a failure, and Friedlaender's conflictual relationship with his father was exacerbated. When Friedlaender finished his third year in high school, his father found a position for him in an insurance firm and hoped that his son would begin a career as a businessman. But now Friedlaender's chronic asthma forced him to travel to a sanitorium near Genoa, where he spent two years recovering. During this time, he developed an interest in Schopenhauer and especially authors whom he called bizarre: Lucian, De Quincey, Poe, Rabelais, Swift, Sterne, Jean Paul, and Paul Scheerbart. Upon his return from Italy in 1891, he decided to resume his high school studies to attain the *Abitur*, the German diploma necessary for admission to the university. After two years of private tutoring, he finally received the *Abitur* at the late age of twenty-three and immediately enrolled in the school of medicine at the Ludwig-Maximilian University in Munich, where Oskar Panizza had also studied. In fact, Panizza had published his story "The Operated Jew" that same year and was still living in Munich at the time Friedlaender began his studies. There is, however, no indication that Friedlaender ever met Panizza, though he probably became aware of Panizza's notorious trial.

By the spring of 1895, Friedlaender moved to Berlin to study, first dentistry and then philosophy. Friedlaender's father was extremely disappointed that his son had abandoned his study of medicine, but he had resigned himself by this time to the fact that his son was drawn more to contemplative, intellectual life than to science. Indeed, Friedlaender underwent a major spiritual crisis in 1897 that he considered the turning point of his life.

> At that time, the ethical problem began to occupy my thoughts more intensively. Until then I had remained amoral without any misgivings in order to be able to do what I wanted to do without conflicts, even though my conscience often had great trouble in dissolving the burden of my moral nightmares. . . . While studying certain chapters of physics at school, especially Schopenhauer's theory of color followed by Goethe's theory, I came across the formula of polarity. It seemed to me that it mysteriously contained the meaning of life. I had tasted the affirmation of life as a pole only much too drastically. In order to make my decision I also had to experience the opposite pole. Due to these internal experiments and guided by an ascetic intention as well, I almost completely forgot to eat and drink for weeks and experienced fantastic ecstasies. These raptures contained visions of a polar life in which my floating "I" moved more and more blazingly like the sun between all the poles of life, between the yes and no of the will. I conceived a philosophy, which I called "On the Live Indifference of the Polarity of the World."[4]

Although he was to elaborate this philosophy in greater detail under the influence of Kant and the German neo-Kantians in Berlin, Friedlaender's basic moral and intellectual disposition, especially the mystical side, which was more radically developed during his Paris exile, now became clear. Having finally reached the point of making a commitment, Friedlaender dedicated himself to philosophy. From 1897 to 1899 he studied at the University of Jena. He became deeply upset by his father's death in 1898, especially since they had never resolved their differences. His mother having died eight years before his father, Friedlaender was now dependent on his stepmother for financial support. To make himself more independent, he moved to Frankfurt in

1899 to do research on his doctoral dissertation and to prepare himself for his examinations. While visiting his brother-in-law, the Rabbi Salomon Samuel, in Essen, he made the acquaintance of the neo-Kantian philosopher Ernst Marcus, who was to exercise the most profound influence on Friedlaender's philosophical thinking. At that time, Friedlaender's main goal, however, was to finish his dissertation on Schopenhauer and obtain his doctorate, which he did in 1902. Soon thereafter, Friedlaender wrote his first book about the natural scientist Robert Julius Mayer and began publishing poems in various magazines. For the first time in his life he began earning money. He also had to decide where he would settle down. Since he now felt "modern" and had broken away from Schopenhauer's asceticism with the help of Nietzsche, he of course chose Berlin, which was the avant-garde cultural center of Germany, and which was to be his home from 1906 to 1933.

The year after he made this decision was an extremely productive one for Friedlaender, and it indicated the direction that he was going to take as writer, philosopher, and public speaker. He published four books dealing with logics, psychology, Jean Paul and Schopenhauer,[5] began working as a professional lecturer, and wrote several bizarre stories, which he called *Grotesken*. He also started moving in the Bohemian and literary circles of Berlin. During the next several years he made the acquaintance of such leading intellectuals as Georg Simmel, Martin Buber, and Gustav Landauer, and important writers such as Else Lasker-Schüler, Paul Scheerbart, Erich Mühsam, and Kurt Hiller, and played a major role in the early expressionist movement. Aside from publishing a book of poems entitled *Through Blue Haze* (*Durch blaue Schleier*, 1908), he became known for his grotesque stories, which he first placed in various innovative journals such as *Das Theater, Aktion*, and *Sturm*. With his first book publication of these stories, *Rosa the Beautiful Policeman's Wife* (*Rosa die schöne Schutzmannsfrau*, 1913), Friedlaender established himself on the Berlin literary scene as one of the major expressionist writers of the day. It was not with his real name, however, but with the pseudonym Mynona that he made a name for himself. Carefully chosen, this pseudonym was closely aligned to a philosophical position, which Friedlaender would seek to realize throughout his life and was best expressed in a dialogue that Mynona created in one of his early stories entitled "Präsentismus": "I am not a human being. I am nobody and everybody, the undifferentiated. If people want to understand me, they must die, must be annihilated like me, undifferentiated. I am he for whom the human being is waiting without clearly knowing it."[6]

Though many of his grotesque stories may seem flip and superficial, most incorporated the philosophical principles that he tried to elaborate in his more scholarly works under his "bourgeois" name Friedlaender. As he commented in his *Autobiography*, "my metaphysical intention was quite strong but the scientific objectively systematic arrangement needed a 'better lance,' if it did not want to get nipped in the bud. Therefore, my philosophically inhibited, repressed and discarded productivity helped itself through wiles that resulted in a grotesque deformed birth." For Friedlaender,

> grotesque distortion is the strength and endurance test for spiritual steadfastness, extensiveness, and elasticity; the test that accounts for the correctness of the metaphysical principle of the creative indifference of polar observance. . . . Of course, these grotesque stories are only the playful surrogate, the shadowy presentiment of the paradisiacally undistorted, of the spiritual wholeness of the genuinely adequate world, of the objective ideal, which should answer equally to "the heaven in us."[7]

Put more succinctly, the way to the ideal synthesis in life was for Friedlaender through distortion, through conceiving polar opposites, a process that eventually engenders harmony. "Creation—this seems to me to be the meaning of life and its aesthetical 'promesse de bonheur': art. Creation means creating distinction, difference, polarity out of indifference, the full being of the innermost self. What was previously trust in God is actually religious self-trust."[8]

To offset the chaos in the world around him, Friedlaender used the grotesque as the means for creating balance and sobriety. And it seemed that his own writing positions set the context for working out the extremes in life: on the one hand, Salomo Friedlaender, the bourgeois writer of philosophical treatises, and on the other, Mynona, the Bohemian artist of the grotesque. Even his personal life seemed to mirror these extremes. In 1911, he married Marie-Luise Schwinghoff, and two years after they had their only child, Heinz-Ludwig, both of whom survived World War II and preserved Friedlaender's posthumous papers. They provided a calm, steady home life for Friedlaender, who kept to a constant but unconventional routine during his years in Berlin. He generally slept until noon and worked in the afternoon. In the evening he would put on a wide-rimmed artist's hat, drape himself in a cape, and arm himself with a cane. Then he would go to a tavern, bar, or private house, where he would either read from his works or participate in discussions. Though not given to small talk, Friedlaender was a remarkable orator and had a large following of friends and admirers. He had numerous affairs and was regarded somewhat of a literary celebrity. Although he enjoyed this status, he rarely compromised himself in his writing by playing up to socialites, cliques, or intellectuals with great reputations. Friedlaender remained his own person which led him into conflict with the government, politicians, and various authors such as Erich Maria Remarque, Kurt Tucholsky, Sigmund Freud, Thomas Mann, and Ernst Bloch.[9]

His most important collections of grotesque stories were *Black-White-Red* (*Schwarz-Weiß-Rot*, 1916), *My Papa and the Virgin of Orleans* (*Mein Papa und die Jungfrau von Orléans*, 1921), *The Strike of the Trappists* (*Der Trappistenstreik*, 1922), and *The Railroad Accident or The Anti-Freud* (*Das Eisenbahnunglück oder der Anti-Freud*, 1925). He also published fascinating novellas and novels such as *Under the Sheet of the Corpse* (*Unterm Leichentuch*, 1920), *The Creator* (*Der Schöpfer*, 1920), *Grey Magic* (*Graue Magie*, 1922), and *Tarzianade* (1924).[10] Almost all these works were iconoclastic, heretical, and provocative and served to illustrate his unusual philosophical notions fully developed in his most significant scholarly work, *Creative Indifference* (*Schöpferische Indifferenz*, 1918). For example, he himself asserted in an aphorism from this book that "the artist objectivizes; but the philosopher creates the creator in himself: he objectivizes the essential requirements of all the possibilities of objectivity and, in this way, the genuine object. Philosophy is that which makes art possible."

Of course, it was a particular kind of philosophy that made art possible, and an art that tended toward harmony. For Friedlaender, art was a magical process which could not be defined, but the position that the artist had to attain could be defined and was put forth in *Creative Indifference*. As he remarked,

"Know yourself!" is the key to magic, that is to the personal will of the world, to one's own divinity, to the individual. One's own self is neutral greatness, mocking all difference in itself but objectifying it. . . . The magical wit of genuine self-recognition is constituted in the neutralization of all objective difference. But this freedom from all difference is what first releases all difference in a harmonious way. The free will is only effective for its objectivization. And all necessity is only objectivized freedom and thus polar.[11]

Never one to shy away from conflicts, Friedlaender sought to justify throughout his book his own difference and marginality in ethical principles that were bound to Kant's notion of the categorical imperative. It is not clear whether the emphasis placed on respect for differences had anything to do with his being Jewish and his desire to overcome the anti-Semitism that had become more intense in Germany after World War I. What is clear, however, is that there was a strong Jewish connection to Kant at that time, and that Friedlaender had close contact with most of the leading Jewish neo-Kantians, for he shared their concern in secularizing Jewish ethics. As George Mosse has pointed out,

> the specific Jewish religious heritage was transformed into ethical idealism and directed toward bringing about a change in present society. Respect for the individual was the essential attitude the categorical imperative demanded, and this again fitted into the pattern of Jewish development. The Jews were increasingly embattled against the effort to view them as a cohesive, evil group, to transform the individual Jew into a stereotype. The pervasiveness of racial thought before and after the war made this battle of prime concern to every Jew. The individualism in neo-Kantian socialism must have had an especially strong appeal under these circumstances, together with the optimistic belief that idealism could be awakened in every man, Jew and Gentile alike.[12]

In particular, it was the optimistic and utopian feature of neo-Kantianism that Friedlaender sought to preserve during the 1920s. In an almost messianic way, Friedlaender felt compelled to spread his peculiar version of Kant's ethics in his fiction and nonfiction. He gave readings of his grotesque tales in literary societies and cafes and broadcast them on the radio. He revised a second edition of *Creative Indifference* and sought to spread the gospel of Kant á la Marcus. He published essays and stories in various journals and cultivated an enormous circle of friends and acquaintances with whom he shared his ideas.[13] Aside from attacking hypocrisy and conformism in German society, he specifically targeted the totalitarian nature of Nazism with his mockery and consequently became a target of the Nazis himself.

Even after he was forced to flee the Nazis in 1933, Friedlaender did not abandon hope that reason and ethics would triumph. He began writing for the German emigrant newspaper *Pariser Tageblatt*, and aside from publishing the optimistic volume of grotesque stories, *The Laughing Job*, in 1935, he worked assiduously on his last major philosophical treatise, *The Magical I (Das magische Ich)* and maintained a massive correspondence, which indicated not only his grave concern about fascism but also a growing spiritual self-contentment.

Among his letters of this period there is one which is worth citing in detail because it reveals his sentiments about Jews and anti-Semitism and also shows a remarkable equanimity at a time when the ground beneath him was eroding. Friedlaender had evidently been given an issue of the *Neue Weltbühne*, which had printed Kurt Tucholsky's suicide letter, and he comments in his own letter to his friend Fritz Lemke that Tucholsky took his life because he became disoriented, had allowed himself to be misled by the fashions of modernity and Fordism, and had abandoned reason. Here some background material about Tucholsky's suicide is necessary.[14]

As I have already indicated, Friedlaender and Tucholsky, who was one of the more brilliant satirical writers of the Weimar period, knew each other well, and though they admired each other, they had also exchanged barbs on different occasions. Both were known for their extraordinary wit, and both sought to expose the hypocrisy of the German bourgeoisie, Tucholsky with acrimonious barbs that were deadly; Friedlaender with burlesque distortions that were disarming. Both came from upper-class Jewish families, but Tucholsky had great difficulties with his "Jewishness" and was ashamed of being associated with Jews, while Friedlaender had no difficulty identifying himself as a Jew, despite the fact that he had no strong ties to the Jewish religion or community. Early in his career as a writer, Tucholsky made a point of "seceding" from Judaism and created a fictional character named Wendriner, who was at the center of various bitter and humorous stories in the 1920s that mocked the pretensions of "Germanized" Jews and made Jewish intellectuals (including Friedlaender) extremely uneasy. It was apparent to many that Tucholsky was caught up in Jewish self-hatred,[15] and this predicament may have been one of the contributing factors that led him to commit suicide on December 19, 1935 in Sweden. Shortly before his death, he had written a letter to the gifted Austrian Jewish writer Arnold Zweig, venting his spleen against the German Jews once more. Not only did he condemn Zionism and call Palestine an English colony, but he argued that Jews had never fought for their emancipation, were essentially cowards, and deserved to spend the rest of their lives in ghettos.

> Whoever does not have freedom in his blood, whoever does not feel what this is, freedom, will never attain it. Whoever accepts the ghetto from the beginning as something given will remain in it eternally. And here and only here is where the failure of the entire German emigration is situated, something that I do want to turn into a Jewish question—here is their guilt, their wretchedness, their misery. That is nothing.[16]

Despite Tucholsky's protestations, his letter was about the "Jewish question" and was used against Jews; after the Communists published it in the *Neue Weltbühne*, the Nazis were able to reprint it in an abridged form that stressed its anti-Semitic features. Of course, for Friedlaender, Tucholsky's letter was totally offensive not only because of its anti-Semitic remarks but because of its irrationalism. He therefore took Tucholsky to task in his own letter to Lemke:

> Reason is neither German nor Jewish, but German as well as Jewish people would do well especially now if they would finally adapt their Germanness or Jewishness to reason. But, Tucholsky says, one *cannot* at all withdraw from one's Jewishness! Ecce homo . . . only Hitler people can talk like that. Indeed, Tucholsky admits that his withdrawal was infantile. Incidentally his nose must have already been sick at that time if he had not smelled the anti-Semitism that was lurking everywhere. He, Tucholsky, did not reveal his identity. . . .
>
> To be sure, Tucholsky does not belong to the "well-known" Jewish anti-Semites, but he is typical of them. Indeed, this is because he, like Hitler, is sensorial and smuggles ethnology from natural sciences into ethics—like a charlatan to top it all off. What is Judaism really? Monotheism, which is actually the most intimately related of all the confessions to the Kantian religion of reason. Even if Kant himself did not notice this, it was *not* the fault of Judaism . . . Just like the Christian emancipation, the Jewish one has had its heroes and heroic martyrs. It is most foolish and ignorant to deny that. Especially today, it is shameless to depict the matter as if something in the *character* of the Jews had caused the ghetto. Certainly, not every Jew is Mendelssohn or like his Platonic idea—Nathan the Wise. But what this Wendriner-Tucholsky does is vulgar empiricism and damaging in a sensory way. Certain Jews do not smell good to him—in a wink *the* Jew is fabricated out of them just like the mob loves to do it. "Ghetto is not a consequence!—Ghetto is fate." He wants to say it is due to the *character* of the Jews. This Jewish character is an empirical product of the mob. I was not born to defend Jews. But I shall defend the sublime, beautiful, good, pious, intelligent *human be-ing* that is just as much in the German as it is in the Negro and

the Jew. I do not continually ask, like Hitler and Tucholsky, whether a human being is empirically and materially Jewish. It may be very interesting ethnologically, even though this science has not yet been fully developed. Humanly, politically, logically, and intellectually it is something a mob would do.[17]

During his exile Friedlaender kept returning to the Jewish question, but it was always placed in the context of humanity and enlightenment. For instance, in a letter to the Salomon family written in 1942, he stated: "The genuine Jew is the purest starting point for the free human being. Marcus was the first one to make Kant applicable, concrete, practical, alive. Before anyone else it is the Jew who gets to the I-helio-center, to the immanent and only divine human, to the pure man of reason like Kant's friend Marcus and later Ludwig Goldschmidt."[18]

Friedlaender never gave up hope that the enlightened and ethical features of the Jewish religion would help pave the way to a more humane civilization. It is remarkable if not baffling how he kept a balanced perspective on the developments in Germany and could even distance himself from what happened to his own life. In the midst of poverty and danger, Friedlaender wrote,

the actual miracle of my life and every human being's life revealed itself to me first in my sixty-fifth year, when I finally discovered the magic formula of *critical* polarism. I uncovered the core of all human evil full of worm holes (the greatest evil is guilt, the demonic) in self-neglect, that is, in the heteronomization (the enslavement) of the I, of the inner self, so that the outside became master of it, the slave became master of his master, the definitely autonomous I. Kant and Marcus had shaken this autonomy of the noumenon out of its sleep. But even they had not attained the restlessness of this self-contemplation, and that is why they had really conveyed very little. They had cancelled out the dependency of the autonomous *Vernunft-Ich* from nature to be sure in a practical way but not yet in a real way.[19]

In his unpublished book *Der magische Ich*, he went on to say: "These pages make only one single, basic insight possible: our 'I' may otherwise be what it wants—but a priori, spontaneous, active forming, transcendental, noumenal, objectively effective, it is the central sun, the support and connection of human life without which neither recognition, action, art, nor faith is possible."[20]

The more Friedlaender's outside world disintegrated, the more he withdrew, but not into a state of depression. For example, in the summer of 1939, René Schickele intervened on Friedlaender's behalf with Thomas Mann, who had played a major role in bringing numerous German intellectuals to America and thus saving their lives. However, in this case, Thomas Mann refused because of the insulting manner in which Friedlaender had mocked him in the 1920s. "I don't like Mynona," he wrote, "and I don't wish to see him here. His way of speaking about 'supposed' Hitler enemies, who do not share his Kantianism, is also highly unpleasant. Let him write his 'decisive' things. By the way why is it that his voice has been 'choked' since '39?"[21] Yet Friedlaender did not become bitter or morbid when he realized that there would be no possibility of escaping the Nazis, who occupied Paris in 1940. From that point onward, he rarely left his apartment. His son eventually escaped to Switzerland, and his wife, who was not Jewish, managed to scrimp and save so that they might survive. By the spring of 1943, Friedlaender became so ill that he could not leave his bed. When the French Gestapo finally came to "deport" him, they realized they would not be able to move Friedlaender and instead took his wife to a camp outside Paris. She was able to prove that she was an Aryan from Berlin and returned to her husband within a matter of weeks.

Though impoverished and bed-ridden, Friedlaender lived to see the end of the war and kept writing with gusto. One of his last essays, written in 1946, was a review of a book by Sartre in which he spoke out against existentialism in the name of Kant's humanism. His spirit may have been indomitable, but his body finally succumbed. He was buried in the Jewish section of the Pantin cemetery in the north of Paris.

It would be interesting to speculate why, in 1922, Friedlaender had felt compelled to write "The Operated Goy" as a response to Oskar Panizza's "The Operated Jew" of some thirty years before. There are no clues in his letters or posthumous papers that provide an answer. However, we do know that "The Operated Jew" had been reprinted in 1914 in *Visionen der Dämmerung* and in 1919 in *Die Welt-Literatur*, a widely distributed newspaper, and that some of Friedlaender's acquaintances such as Gustav Landauer, Tucholsky, and Alfred Kubin, all assimilated Jews, were admirers of Panizza's work. It is highly probable that Friedlaender became aware of Panizza's stories long before he wrote "The Operated Goy." Indeed, the "Panizza Case" had intrigued many writers and critics in the early part of the twentieth century, and Friedlaender had been in Munich at the time Panizza was making a name for himself.

Yet, the question remains: what happened during the early 1920s to prompt Friedlaender to respond to Panizza so late? Was the response really to Panizza or to the ominous signs in Germany at that time? If we recall, the Jews were held responsible by many Germans for the Empire's defeat in World War I, and a new wave of anti-Semitism was on the rise. Professional armies of right-wing mercenaries and the Free Corps stamped out work-ers' uprising and movements for greater democracy and pre-vented socialist organizations from gaining power. Here, too, Jews were often associated with communism and chaos. The only way that the Social Democrats, who had abandoned socialist reform, could maintain control of the government and the popu-lace was through violent means and constant compromises with the conservative forces that represented authoritarianism and traditional class hierarchy. Under attack from the Left and the Right during a period of enormous economic inflation, the Wei-mar Republic and the Social Democratic government barely survived. In fact, one of its most prominent members did not. This was Walter Rathenau, the foreign minister, who, as wealthy Jew and committed Social Democrat, symbolized the betrayal of Germany by the Jews because he had supported war reparations and later the Rapallo Treaty.[22] Rathenau was assassinated on June 24, 1922, and his death sent tremors through liberal and left-wing Jewish circles.

It is interesting to note that there may be a connection here between Tucholsky's response to Rathenau's death and Fried-laender's to Panizza. The first Wendriner story, which appeared in July 6, 1922, expressed Tucholsky's contempt for German Jews, whom he charged with acquiring the worst "German" traits of obsequiousness, provincialism, and authoritarianism in order to advance in society. Wendriner was the *successful* operated Jew. That is, unlike Panizza's Faitel, Wendriner suc-ceeded in becoming totally Germanized and losing his integrity. In all the Wendriner stories he apes everything German, and the satiric Tucholsky makes it appear that Wendriner pitifully stands for the goal of every assimilated Jew.

If we can assume that Friedlaender wrote "The Operated Goy" after reading Tucholsky's first Wendriner story, it makes good sense that he wanted to reply to Tucholsky via a response to Panizza. And, even if this was not the case, it is clear that he, too, was highly disturbed by Rathenau's death and the rise of anti-Semitism and Nazism, as some of his other stories in *Trappistenstreik* (1922) indicate. In one way or the other, Friedlaender was replying to Tucholsky. This reply has some highly unusual features to it that pose a solution to the negative German-Jewish symbiosis.

If one can speak about intent in "The Operated Goy," then it is important to clarify that Friedlaender did *not* intend to denigrate gentiles or celebrate Jews in a response *designed as a laugh*. In fact, the narrative framework of the story is intended to bring about cathartic laughter in his readers. Friedlaender has the anonymous Mynona tell a story in which a certain fictitious Dr. Friedlaender attains the final laugh by minimizing racial differences and thus debunking nationalism and anti-Semitism. It is through laughter, then, that the author Friedlaender wants to undermine prejudice and violence, and this laughter is predicated to a great extent on self-mockery, for he also pokes fun at himself throughout the story. Friedlaender stressed the importance of such mockery in *Creative Indifference*:

> The creator is also the creator of his self-mockery; even frivolity is the creature of the creator. The creative principle is, more than anything else, laughter! The humorless divinity, holiness, the serious ceremoniousness and dignity, the rigid majesty of the ruling principle are lifeless self-misunderstandings. Life laughs, and it would be objectively so sad to stop it being so when it were subjectively cheerful. A god, who cannot get the best of himself, a serious religion making life miserable, they make a stiff cardboard death out of life. The externally laughing cheerfulness of one's own divinity ultimately penetrates everything. Its laughter is absolute, sublime above all the relative laughing of the creature. All

seriousness is only the theme of laughter. The art of living is cheerful; the serious life is not art. The divine principle is only morbid until one has become the principle oneself.[23]

Interestingly, Friedlaender chooses a woman, Rebecca Gold-Isaac, to be the most active principle of laughter in his narrative. Not only is she the "other" as Jew but also as female/witch/princess, for she literally tempts and seduces Count Reshok to transform himself into a Jew. It is only by recognizing the other, Friedlaender implies, that reconciliation of extremes can be reached. Moreover, Rebecca realizes that "whoever hates and despises predisposes himself in all secrecy, slowly but surely, for the most intimate ties of blood, indeed, for an identification with the object of his negation."

Throughout the narrative there are puns that play with traditional expectations and provide options to stereotypical thinking. In addition, there are reversals in the behavior of the characters and the plot, intended to expose prejudice and dogmatism and to make readers laugh. For example, Rehsok becomes Kosher, and instead of having five Teutonic children, his children are named Shlaume, Shmul, Feigelche, Pressel and Yankef. His first name Kreuzwendedich is a pun and means "cross, turn around." His bodyguard Bor turns against the Borussians to defend the Jews. Rebecca Gold-Isaac's name is a grotesque stereotypical equation of Jewishness with wealth, and her father is a mock version of the "super Jew." Rehsok's family, too, is changed from the respectable anti-Semitic and nationalistic clan into the laughing stock of the Aryan upper-classes.

It is precisely at the points of the extremes in life, the polarities, that Friedlaender believed there was hope. In this regard, Rebecca and Rehsok constitute the opposite poles of the *same* whole. They can only be reconciled, however, when they recognize how they are related to each other, and together they pose the possibility for harmony and an ethical ideal. Ironically, Rebecca and Rehsok are moved to change because they are so polarized, or as Mynona ironically puts it: "Anti-Semitism is perhaps even more Jewish than Judaism." Rebecca changes her name and transforms her hate into love for Rehsok, who, of course, undergoes a more radical transformation than Rebecca. His operation is more necessary than her change because of the negative symbiosis between Germans and Jews and the domination of Germans over Jews. That is, in order for the world to be transformed the German must become Jew, or as Friedlaender argues on a more general basis, racial difference is not to serve as the basis for making decisions and distinctions in life—a position that Rebecca holds from the very beginning.

For Friedlaender, as we have seen, the Jew was the starting point for the free human being. This viewpoint may seem somewhat biased if not racist, but Friedlaender did not mean that there was something essential about Jews that made them better human beings. Nor did he believe that there was something essential in Jewish identity that distinguished Jews from other people. Rather, he was concerned with the ethical principles in the Jewish *religion* and thought that they were the basis for universal enlightened thought and behavior. Ultimately, the Jewish categories had to become "anonymous," but before that could happen, the "joke" was that the world had to become Jewish or transformed into its opposite. Domination had to be resisted by laughter, and "Dr." Friedlaender's operations within Mynona's story are symbolically related to Friedlaender's own operations with his pen, performed to induce laughter. Implicit in the total operations of the narrative is a philosophy that would allow for the toleration of difference and individuality.

Though Friedlaender's philosophical position may seem somewhat ludicrous, especially because of its mystical leanings, his grotesque stories must be taken seriously because they reveal to what extent our actions and words are still based on anti-Semitism, racism, and our need to dominate. Our pathology is that we do not know how to laugh. Friedlaender's stories are part of a deeply ingrained dialogue about Germans and Jews that transcends both Germans and Jews. Certainly, Rebecca is Jewish, but she is also the Other—the woman, the person of color, the poor. She is the figure who is "normally" operated on in Western society so that she must surrender her particularity. This is directly related to contemporary problems caused by modernity and the Holocaust, as we have seen in Zygmunt Bauman's work, and it is all the more reason why Friedlaender's "Operated Goy" has such iconic significance.

Friedlaender's story is in some respects a sign of our times. Yet his work, along with Panizza's "The Operated Jew," has left a heritage that few writers want to assume because of the incendiary nature of the subject matter. However, there is one important writer, who has dare to pursue the theme in direct relation to Panizza and Friedlaender. I am thinking of Edgar Hilsenrath, a German-Jewish writer, who wrote an intriguing picaresque novel entitled *The Nazi and the Barber* in 1977. The anti-hero of this grotesque novel is Max Schulz, alias Itzig Finkelstein. Born a bastard on May 23, 1907 in the small city of Wieshalle, Schulz, frog-eyed, short, and dark, grows up in Anton Slavitski's barbershop, where he is often beaten and subjected to the beastly lovemaking of his mother Minna and Anton. One of his best friends is Itzig Finkelstein, blond, blue-eyed and tall, whose father Chaim owns the best barbershop in Wieshalle which is called "Der Herr von Welt" and which is opposite Slavitski's shop. Schulz's dream is to own a shop like Chaim's one day, but in the meantime he must tolerate the crude conditions in Slavitski's shop. When the Hitler regime begins, he becomes a member of the SS and eventually a guard at the concentration camp Laubwalde, where 200,000 Jews are murdered, among them Chaim and Itzig Finkelstein, whom he personally kills. Pursued as a mass murderer when the war comes to an end, Schulz switches his identity in Berlin and becomes Itzig Finkelstein. He has a concentration camp number tattooed on his arm and lets himself be circumcised. He reads books about Jewish religion and history, and officials declare him to be Itzig Finkelstein. After working as a dealer on the black market for a few years, Schulz decides that the future as a Jew looks better in Israel. So he leaves on the ship Exitis, and during the voyage he carries on imaginary discussions with Itzig Finkelstein.

> Dear Itzig. They say that one hates what one wants to deny. I, Itzig Finkelstein, at one time Max Schulz, always looked like a Jew . . . even though that's not true. But they said it. Yet, they said it: he looks like a Jew!
> Think about it, Itzig. Just for this reason I should have hated you. In order to deny something that's not me. . . . merely because I was afraid that I could be it. Or, because they believed that I was it even though I knew that I wasn't it. Do you understand that?
> You see then. You understand it. Me, too. In spite of it all I've never hated you. Strange . . . huh? But it's true. I, Itzig Finkelstein, at one time Max Schulz, didn't hate Jews.[24]

After arriving in Israel, Schulz finds a job in Schmuel Schmulevitsch's barbershop in a small town outside Tel Aviv. Aside from fighting with an Israeli terrorist group against the British forces and with the Haganah, Schulz becomes a respected Zionist and barber. In fact, he becomes such a perfect Jew that, toward the end of his life, after he finally has his own barbershop, he cannot convince a retired judge that he really was the mass murderer Max Schulz. He dies of a heart attack in 1968 even though, or because the doctors try a transplant operation with the heart of a rabbi.

Hilsenrath's novel is a fascinating if not macabre exploration of the stereotypes both Germans and Jews have of one another.[25] What appears to be a perfect Jew is a mass murderer, an operated German, who cannot shed his Jewishness and yet cannot be saved by a Jewish heart. Schulz's ironic autobiography explodes the traditional German and Jewish stereotypes and compels the reader to rethink German-Jewish operations from 1907 to 1968, for nobody is what he or she appears in the novel. In fact, the more Schulz becomes the Other, the more difficulty he has in regaining a sense of his German identity. It even appears that his punishment, the only just punishment for Germans, is to become "Jewish" or the Other. By becoming Jewish, Schulz is no longer a danger to himself or others. He gradually comes to feel and act as the Other, thereby breaking down and exploding the stereotypes that drove him to become a murderer.

The obvious link between Hilsenrath and Friedlaender is in the grotesque humor they use to minimize their fear of the Other, namely the German, creating the conditions for tolerance through laughter. On the other hand, Panizza is deadly serious about annihilating the Jew, despite the ambivalent attitude toward the Other he expresses in his story. There is very little to laugh about in "The Operated Jew," for his narrative strategy points to extermination not transformation as a solution to overcoming difference. Friedlaender thought he found the recipe for the resolution of differences in laughter and creative indifference, and though he may have been deceiving himself, there is paradoxically something distinctive in his endeavor to become anonymous and subvert the operations of domination. Until the subversion is complete, that is, until we learn to resist domination through empathy and laughter, Friedlaender suggests, we shall never know ourselves. Nor can we know ourselves until we stop imposing our will on others and reconcile polarities. In this regard, the "operated goy" and the "laughing Job" become ethical models in Friedlaender's utopian vision of a world too shortsighted to see where it is headed.

Notes

1. Mynona, *Der lachende Hiob und andere Grotesken* (Paris: Editions du Phénix, 1935). Subsequent citations appear in the text.

2. See *Ich—Autobiographische Skizze (1871–1936)*. This is a typewritten manuscript among the posthumous papers located in the Deutsches Literaturarchiv/Schiller-Naionalmuseum in Marbach. Parts of it were published in Hans Daiber, *Vor Deutschland wird gewarnt* (Gütersloh: Sigbert Mohn, 1967): 35–44, and in Mynona, *Rosa die schöne Schutzmannsfrau und andere Grotesken*, ed. Ellen Otten (Zurich: Arche, 1965): 201–34.

    My remarks in this section will be based in part on Friedlaender's own writings and on the exhaustive research done by the following scholars: Joseph Strelka, "Mynona" in *Expressionismus als Literatur* (Bern: Francke, 1969): 623–36; Manfred Kuxdorf, "Salomo Friedlaender, Mynona: Werk und Wirkung. Forschungsbericht," *Zeitgeschicte* 5 (1977): 95–105; Hartmut Geerken, "Nachwort" in Mynona, *Prosa. Der Schöpfer, Tarzaniade, Der antibabylonische Turm*, ed. Geerken, vol. 2 (Munich: Edition Text + Kritik, 1980): 277–318; Hartmut Geerken, ed., *Salomo Friedlaender. Mynona. Briefe aus dem Exil* (Mainz: Von Hase und Koehler Verlag, 1982); and Peter Cardorff, *Friedlaender (Mynona) zur Einführung* (Hamburg: SOAK, 1988).

3. Mynona, *Rosa die schöne Schutzmannsfrau und andere Grotesken*, 205–6.

4. Mynona, *Rosa*, 222–23.

5. See *Logik: Die Lehre vom Denken.* (Berlin: Hillger Verlag, 1907); *Psychologie: Die Lehre von der Seele* (Berlin: Hilger Verlag, 1907); *Jean Paul as Denker: Gedanken aus seinen sämtlichen Werken* (Munich: Piper, 1907); *Schopenhauer: Seine Persönlichkleit in seinen Werken*, 2 vols. (Stuttgart: Lutz Verlag, 1907).

6. "Präsentismus. Rede des Erdkaisers an die Menschen," *Der Sturm* 3 (1912/13): 253.

7. "Salomo Friedlaender (Mynona)" in *Vor Deutschland wird gewarnt,* 40–41.

8. "Salomo Friedlaender (Mynona)" in *Vor Deutschland wird gewarnt,* 42.

9. See *Der Antichrist und Ernst Bloch* (Munich: Kurt Wolff, 1920); *Hat Erich Maria Remarque wirklich gelebt?* (Berlin: Paul Steegemann, 1929).

10. For a succinct summary of Mynona's works, see Manfred Kuxdorf, "Salomo Friedlaender, Mynona: Werk und Wirkung. Forschungsbericht."

11. *Schöpferische Indifferenz* (Munich: Georg Müller, 1918), 416.

12. "Left-Wing Intellectuals in the Weimar Republic" in *Germans and Jews* (New York: Grosset & Dunlap, 1970): 206.

13. Geerken asserts that Friedlaender knew almost all the most significant intellectuals and artists of his period and lists the following people: Herwarth Walden, Paul Scheerbart, Else Lasker-Schüler, Johannes Schlaf, Franz Oppenheimer, Alfred Kubin, Samuel and Ida Lubinski, Ernst Marcus, Rudolf Pannwitz, Otto zur Linde, Martin Buber, Georg Simmel, Erich Mühsam, Ludwig Rubiner, Kurt Hiller, Karl Kraus, Leonhard Frank, Arthur Segal, Udo Rukser, Joseph Roth, Romain Rolland, Ferdinand Hardekopf, Erwin Loewenson, Walter Rheiner, Georg Lukács, Georg Grosz, Raoul Hausmann, Hannah Höch, Ludwig Meidner, Kurt Schwitters, Carl Einstein, Magnus Hirschfeld, René Schickele, André Gide, and David Luschnat. See Mynona, *Prosa,* Vol. 2, 292.

14. For an excellent study of Tucholsky's final years in exile, see Harold L. Poor. *Kurt Tucholsky and the Ordeal of Germany, 1914–1935* (New York: Charles Scribner's Sons, 1968): 203–28.

15. For an extensive and most perceptive analysis of this problem, see Sander L. Gilman, *Jewish Self-Hatred: Anti-Semitism and the Hidden Language of the Jews* (Baltimore: The Johns Hopkins University Press, 1989).

16. Tucholsky, *Politische Briefe,* ed. Fritz J. Raddatz (Reinbek bei Hamburg: Rowohlt, 1969): 119–20.

17. Salomo Friedlaender/Mynona, *Briefe aus dem Exil,* 60–61.

18. *Briefe,* 179.

19. Daiber, *Vor Deutschland wird gewarnt,* 192.

20. Daiber, *Vor Deutschland,* 192.

21. Daiber, *Vor Deutschland,* 189.

22. Cf. Henry Pachter, "Walter Rathenau: Musil's Arnheim or Mann's Naphta," *Weimar Etudes* (New York: Columbia University Press, 1982): 171–88.

23. *Schöpferische Indifferenz*, 468.

24. *Der Nazi & der Friseur* (Cologne: Literarischer Verlag Braun, 1977): 222.

25. For a thorough discussion of stereotypes, see Sander L. Gilman, *Difference and Pathology: Stereotypes of Sexuality, Race, and Madness* (Ithaca: Cornell University Press, 1985).